Jackie Hooks

CHAPTER 1

Broken

In 1981, when I was 6 years old, my sister and I were abducted by a stranger. We were playing alone in the parking lot of my apartment complex. He seemed to walk up out of nowhere. He was not a monster. He was not disgusting. He was a young, good looking guy in Jordache jeans and he was catching bunnies in the woods. There was no fear surrounding the moment he asked us if we wanted to go catch bunnies too. There was zero hesitation. There were bunnies in the woods and this great guy, who seemed like a camp counselor, was going to let us come catch them with him. My sister and I laughed the whole walk to the woods. We talked about how we would have to convince our mom to let us keep the bunnies. We talked about where we would keep them, what we would name them, what color they would be...We weren't walking fast. There was no hurry. There were just two little girls laughing and talking and being so super excited about the possibilities of bunnies.

The minute we walked into the woods there were two blankets on the ground, and the man said that we would have to catch the bunnies with our shirts. The charade was up. The bunnies were a lie. And I froze. I remember taking off my shoes and telling the man that we could catch the bunnies in our shoes. I said that a whole bunch, and then my mind went black and I couldn't move. I don't know how long I stood there frozen. I don't know what happened in between my failed attempt to sway this man with my tennis shoes, and the moment my eyes opened, all I know is that I felt terrified. The man was in my face. He was yelling at me to do things. I wanted to cry, but I was not going to cry for him. I came up to his waist.

He was standing right in front of me. And in the chaos, and in all my fear, life started to move in slow motion. I could see every single detail of a small branch right next to me. I heard a voice inside my head and inside my heart say, "Run or Die." And I ran.

I ran faster than a grown man that day. I ran barefoot. I was 6 years old and as I ran, and as he ran after me, I fell apart. I did not cry. I simply broke. There was a man working on his car, and he stood up shocked as I ran screaming out of the woods that someone had to go get my sister. I had left her behind. I said it again, "A man has my sister in the woods." And he looked at me as though he could not believe what I was saying. And a lie was planted in my mind that instant: He was disgusted with me because I had left my sister with the man in the woods. I hated myself. I was a horrible person. I had failed. I would not cry. I would stand there and wait as he went back into the woods. I would stand, alone, hoping that my sister was coming. I would stand there for what felt like forever wanting more than anything to see my sister's face. I needed to tell her I was sorry I ran. I needed to know she was ok. I needed to see her with her blue shirt with the flowers on the front. I needed to see her. In my memory, the man working on the car carried my sister from the woods. I don't think this part is real, but that is the way that moment felt. When I saw her I could breathe again.

I hate my story. I hate my story because it points out just how broken I am. And I am broken. Really really broken. I can give you all of the Christian vocabulary and tell you that I have been made whole in Christ, and I have. I have been saved and set free. But my story still makes me cry. My story still makes me hope my children live a totally different, benign life. My story still makes people not know what to say to me. And so, it is this uncomfortable truth and, yes, it is powerful. My story is powerful. Because Jesus is big, y'all. The fingerprints of Jesus are I all over my life. But it is still horribly hard to stand completely bare in front of you, and show you where I broke.

My parents divorced when I was four years old. They lived in Nashville, TN in a big old house. My mom was an attorney's wife. My dad was not so happy being an attorney anymore. Things began to fall apart. And my mom went from being a stay-at-home-mom to a struggling- working- mom. We left Nashville on Halloween of 1980. We trick-or-treated at a motel that night. We moved to Arlington, TX where my mom had grown up. We went "home" to be with her family. I remember feeling really really sad that my dad did not want us anymore. I felt sad that my dad did not come with us. I felt sad when I heard the song, "You've Got a Friend", by James Taylor because it made me think of my dad. But things were not going well with my mom, and feeling sad just seemed like the worst thing I could do to anyone. So, I mostly just felt nothing.

We moved into some apartments. They were not the worst, and they were not the best. My mom worked at a library in another city. Every morning she dropped my older sister, Jeannie, and I off at my grandparent's house before school. My grandmother was usually leaving for work, and my grandfather was still asleep. We would watch TV, and eat breakfast. We would try to keep as quiet as possible in the little house because nothing was worse than accidentally waking up my grandfather. My sister left for school early (she was a first grader), and I was home for hours before I went to afternoon kindergarten (back when kindergarten was a half day). Some days my grandfather did not wake up before I left. I watched a lot of TV. I watched "Bewitched", "My Three Sons", "Green Acres", and I would turn it off when "Mr. Ed" came on because that was just stupid. I would think a lot. And I would be quiet. Sometimes I would eat Pepperidge Farm coconut cake right out of the box. Sometimes my grandfather would wake up and make me lunch or watch TV with me. He was in a wheelchair, and would sit in his recliner and smoke cigarettes or swisher sweets. He got angry all the time. He yelled and cussed from his bedroom or the garage where he fixed lawnmowers. He would listen to Elvis sing gospel music while he worked on lawnmowers and yell at anyone within earshot, and that was mostly me. Sometimes I would have to go out to the garage to get his tools, and I was five and had no idea what he was talking about. I would stand there trying to guess with him yelling the names of tools at me while I tried not to cry. I was pretty darn good at not crying by the end of kindergarten. Sometimes he would tell me I was his favorite grandchild. Sometimes I would have to go get the neighbors to help me because he had fallen and I couldn't get him up. Sometimes he would tell me I could take a puff of his cigarettes with him or take a sip of his beer. And sometimes I would. I felt sad and nervous a lot. But when I was good and quiet and compliant everything seemed to go much better. And I loved TV. And I loved going to school.

Every afternoon, another family would come pick me up on their way to school in their truck. It had a mountain scape on the back window. Their daughter, Jessica, and I sat in the back. To this day I have no idea how my mom made this arrangement, but the pick-up truck arrived on my first day of school at Ruby Ray Swift Elementary. I loved everything about kindergarten. I loved my teacher. I loved block center. I loved recess. I loved nap time. I loved the "Letter People" who told all about the alphabet. I loved the library. I loved the bathrooms and the water fountains. I loved seeing my sister in the hall. I loved dismissal and waiting outside school. I can't remember who drove us back to my grandparent's house, but we would go back home and play outside with all the other neighborhood kids who were now home too. This part of my day was wonderful. We played hide and go seek. We made clubs. We found secret passage ways. We rode bikes. Sometimes we would steal my grandfather's wheelchair and push each other down the hill in it. We had cartwheel races. We roller skated. And we only came inside if it rained or if we needed water or if it was time for "The Brady Bunch" reruns. It was fabulous. My mom would pick us up after work, and we would head home to our apartment.

Things were hard. Money was tight. Really tight. My mom was super sad or angry all the time. My sister wanted to go back to Nashville. I wanted my mom to be happy. Little kids are pretty adaptable, and I was just trying to adapt. The kids we played with at our apartment were different than the kids in my grandparent's neighborhood. They cussed a lot. They knew crazy grown up things. Most of them had single moms. We would play in the parking lots or on the stairs. We were poor kids. My mom fed the other kids on most weekends, but that was stressful because our food didn't stretch far. We always ate. It was not ever fancy. We washed our clothes in the sink because the Laundromat was a luxury. We stood in line at the grocery store and put things back until the bill became affordable, and sometimes my mom would start to cry. We had checks that bounced. The girls below us were sent to live in an orphanage when their parents were evicted. Kids stood outside and smoked pot on the weekends. If you went to the pool there was always something crazy happening there. We lived a pretty stereotypical life for kiddos that were growing up poor in apartments with single moms. We were nothing special. We were par for the course.

On November 7th of 1980, my uncle, Randy, gave my sister and I each a Bible. I have no clue why he gave us a Bible on November 7th, but he did. And the only way I know this is because the date is written at the front of the Bible. There was a man (Jesus) on the cover who looked so kind. He was the "Kenny Loggins" rockstar Jesus. He was holding a little girl. I thought she looked just like me. No one ever read that Bible to me. Not one single word. I don't think I even understood what the book was about. Charlton Heston is depicted as Moses on the inside, and sometimes I would flip through the pages and look at the drawings. I loved that book, and I would walk around and tell my mom or my sister, "The man on the front is holding me. It looks just like me on the front, and He is holding me." Jesus handed me the entire gospel before my world broke completely apart. He was there. He was reaching into my darkness. He was trying to put His arms around me through the cover of a book because He loved me so dang much.

By first grade, we had fallen into a routine. We sometimes were in daycare, and when my mom couldn't afford it we were with my grandfather. My mom dated, and went out, and we ate dinner at my grandparent's house a bunch. That was usually less than comfortable, but I liked watching, "Wheel of Fortune" because my grandmother said that I could win if I was ever actually on it. We played with the kids from school and in my grandparent's neighborhood during the week, and with the kids in our apartments on the weekend. There were bright spots like the fact that my mom read to us every night, and going to bookstores, collecting stickers or walking to the "Hi, Neighbor" store to get Laffy Taffy. This was all I knew. My life may have been filled with struggle and alcoholism and anger and sadness, but it was the only life I had known. It was just the way things were, and no one around me ever said anything about it, so, it never seemed that weird. No one was angry at the way my grandfather spoke to us, so, you just assume that is the way you should be spoken to...it doesn't matter what is right or wrong...

When the man in the woods stepped in to take the final blows on a pretty shaky foundation, the damage was devastating. The police were called when we got back to our apartment. The guy working on his car walked us all the way home. No one was looking for us. There were composite sketches made, and the police asked a lot of questions. I remember sitting on the couch being more embarrassed than I have ever been in my life, and thinking people who make composite sketches are really good at what they do. I can close my eyes and still see that sketch. They asked the guy working on his car a million questions too. It felt long and uncomfortable and like we had done something so wrong. Wrong enough that the cops had come. I don't remember my mom hugging us. I don't remember tears of gratefulness that we were ok. I remember feeling really horrible that my mom was upset. Before the cops left, the guy who had worked on his car and brought us home asked if he could pray for us. I remember him praying that Jesus would heal us and protect us. I remember wishing he lived with us, and wondering what we would do now. But nothing happened and nothing changed. We were tucked into bed that night as usual and we never talked about it again. I don't remember ever saying how scared I was, or how much it felt like I was going to die. We did not go to counseling. The police never came back. The counselors at the school never came and checked on us. Life just went on. And since life went on, it seemed like no big deal. And since it seemed like no big deal then I was stupid for letting it scare me so much. And I never cried, and a 6 year old little girl curled up and died somewhere along the way.

I was afraid of the dark. I was afraid to spend the night at other people's houses. I was afraid to go to sleep. I was afraid to walk home from school. I was afraid that someone was always following me. I was afraid that someone was going to murder me. I was afraid that people were watching me. I was afraid all the time. But I never told anyone. I had little disaster plans ready at a moment's notice. What I would say if someone tried to grab me. What I would do if someone tried to grab my sister or my friends. What I would do if someone tried to kill me. What I would do if someone was on the balcony. They never caught the man in the woods, and so, for me, he was still out there all the time waiting to come back and get us. I felt frozen in fear on the inside and there was a need for everything to be ok on the outside because things still weren't good with my mom. She was still sad and angry all the time. My grandfather was still mean and cussing and yelling all the time, and he had taken to calling me, "Fat Jack". Lovely. I was in need of someone seeing me...but no one seemed to see me unless I was funny and happy. So I became funny. And happy. And the kiddo who was good at making adults laugh. It was a good role.

We finally moved out of our apartment when the woman downstairs shot her husband. So, we packed up and moved to a duplex with a stackable washer and dryer. Life was going to get better. We had a backyard. My mom had a boyfriend. We had Rainbow Brite bedspreads. We had the most crazy lavish Christmas the year I was in second grade. Cabbage Patch Kids, Mongoose bikes, my mom got a fur coat, Esprit sweatshirts...everything was the best. Everything was going to be good. My mom changed jobs so she could have more money. We were allowed to ride our bikes to school and ride them back to my grandfather's house. By the time I was in second grade, if my grandfather was screaming from the garage for someone to get him tools or a glass of water, my sister and I would sit inside and wait as long as we could. We would pretend we didn't hear him. Or yell at each other over who had gone to fetch stuff for him last. Or sometimes, if he was really drunk, he would call for my grandmother and she wasn't there so, we would sit and listen to him yell for "Mother" over and over. And then at some point there would be lots of cuss words and we would jump up and act like we had just heard him yelling. It was stupid. But it made it easier, and it was all we could do to have a bit of control. We loved him. He called us his chickadees. But that was yelled really loud and obnoxiously and it was over the top with hugs too tight, and it felt like a lie. He loved us, and then acted like he hated us. He loved us, and then everything we did was wrong. And at some point you just quit believing what anyone says because things are just the way they are, and adults will say anything they want and then act a totally different way. So, people can tell you they love you till they're blue in the face, and you can hug them and say you love them too, but you don't have to believe them because words are words and they are clearly not changing anything.

And my mom's boyfriend wasn't really changing things either. He was an alcoholic. He was a mean drunk. He liked to yell at my mom, and he seemed to like to say he was sorry a bunch too. He would get so mad at the dinner table if my sister was "smacking" her food. He would get so angry if we did not like the escargot he decided he wanted to eat. He would get so angry if we felt sorry for the old lady who lived next door who had had a stroke. He smelled like beer every time he was at our house. And he had no problem whatsoever screaming for hours at me and my sister. I remember thinking that the neighbors could surely hear him. I remember thinking my mom should make him stop. I remember thinking he wasn't my dad and he had no right to do this, but I never said any of those things. I just kept quiet. And when my older sister would yell back at him, or tell him he was wrong, or leave the table in tears, I would tell her to stop. I would want her to sit quiet too so it would end sooner. But she could never do that. She could never lie on the outside. I hated myself for being so fake. I hated myself for siding with him. But it was survival. I could give up myself and all of my feelings to survive. Sometimes I wanted to be more like Jeannie, but mostly, I just wanted everybody to shut up so life could maybe get better. Unfortunately, it was not going to get better for a long time.

I sit here, over 30 years after these events were my life, and I see that Jesus came in the form of teachers. Jesus came in the form of the ladies who taught me five days a week and thought I was smart and creative. Jesus came in the form of the principal of our school, William Bryant, who seemed to adore us, and knew all of our names and cheered for us at Field Days. Jesus came in the form of a janitor, Mr. Brown, who thought we were the best kids ever. Jesus lived in the halls of Swift Elementary in a way that was almost tangible. I did not know it was Him then, but I can look back and see His footprints up and down those halls. Jesus gave me friends who were living their own nightmares too. He gave me my lifelong best friends, Jamie and Judah, who were surviving their own lives too...and

He allowed me to feel "normal" in my sea of absolute insanity. They knew about the man in the woods. They knew how scared and scarred I was. They knew that I hated my mom's boyfriend. They knew that I couldn't stand my grandfather half of the time. They also totally understood how much I loved him. They were playing their own games, and surviving their own lives, so there was no judgement at all if you had to give up all of your values just to make it through a day. Or if you simply had to be sane because no one else was being anywhere near sane. Or if you felt like you were an adult even though you were only 8. Or if you hated kids who complained about little things like not getting what they wanted for their birthday, or not getting to watch their favorite TV shows, or wanting to sit by certain person at school because that was all stupid and you, you knew there were real things to be upset about in the world. And I can look back and see that Jesus was there. He was there in all the people who kept telling me I was special. He was there in the teachers who said that I was smart. He was there year after year, and I had that dang Bible. And it now sits on my writing desk as a reminder that He was there all along.

My mom, Peggy, was not a bad person. She was not actively trying to make life hard for us or pick the worst people to influence us. My grandfather raised her. This was her father. So, she was the daughter of an alcoholic who had escaped it all and moved to Tennessee, married an attorney, lived the good life...and it all fell apart. My mom loved us ferociously. But when you are a struggling single mom who is heartbroken and drowning in bills...When you are sick and no one offers to take over with the kids...when you are having to make choices that all revolve around money...Choices get made. You do the best you can. But sometimes, it seems like the only people who are willing to reach into your darkness and lend a helping hand are people who are living in darkness too. My mom served on PTA. She got a scholarship so we could go to the YMCA and play sports. She packed our lunches (even though we qualified for free lunch...she would never fill out the form). If there was not enough food, she didn't eat. She always had good clothes for us. She made our birthday cakes each year and would decorate them to look like whatever we wanted. She was trying. But sometimes it seems that the ones who could really help, really make a difference, wouldn't walk the distance to the other side of town and see this woman as someone drowning. All they saw was a woman making poor choices. It's easier to talk about her than to talk with her. But my mom grew up the daughter of an alcoholic, so faking like you're ok came easy to her and she was a pro when we were in public. She was gorgeous and young and smart and funny. And I wonder, if while she dated her horrible boyfriend for two years, if her self esteem had plummeted and if she had begun to wonder if she was worth anyone's time at all. I wonder if being back home with her father and all of his words of disappointment began to be the nails in her coffin. I wonder if settling seemed like the only option. You make choices. It's not the best, but we could eat better. It's not the best, but I could put the girls in day care. It's not the best, but we could pay our bills. But eventually, her boyfriend left too. And my mom was coming undone.

I kept a letter from her boyfriend for years. It was a long letter about how sorry he was for yelling at me all the time. How sorry he was for all the mistakes he had made. How much he wanted to be my dad. It made me cry to read it. It made me cry because he only wrote it to me. There was no letter for my sister who took the brunt of his abuse. We were not his children. He did not love us both the same. He loved the compliant child who was chubby and funny. The wickedly smart child who would give him back as much as he dished out was not so adorable. But man, I wished I could be as brave as her. But this was survival and I was surviving. When he left I was happy. I thought my mom was going to marry him. I thought this was going to be my life forever. And even though I offered lots of hugs and I love you's and let me spend quality time with you and ride around in the back of your El Camino...it was all a lie, and I hated him. I hated him. I hated him for every sleepless night. I hated him for the way he talked to my mom and my sister. I hated him for being drunk and passed out on our couch. I hated him for the days I walked home from school and he was in our living room with his friends doing drugs and I was alone and uncomfortable and had to act like I didn't notice. And I never told my mom, and I only told Jamie and Judah because they would understand why I wouldn't tell my mom or teachers or the police...those suggestions were for kids who complained about not sitting next to their friends at lunch...not for people surviving.

I have a friend, Amy McGown, my former counselor, who told me that Satan is a skilled predator. I had heard this before. The Bible tells us that Satan is like a lion prowling around and waiting to devour us. But Amy said it a little different. Amy said once, in one of my counseling sessions, decades after being a student at Ruby Ray Swift Elementary, a good predator, a good hunter, lines up their kill. A good hunter sets a target on their prey...either through a scope on their gun or through their eyes, but they will line up their kill with a target on them. Amy believes that since Satan is a skilled hunter, hunting for each of us as we live our lives, he places a target on us long before he ever tries to destroy us. This target is the lies we come to believe. I have had a target on me most of my life saying that I am not important. This target was placed there by the absolute vacant relationship with my father. This target was placed on me when no one stood up for me when my grandfather verbally and emotionally abused me. This target was fastened into place when my mother allowed her boyfriend to say whatever he wanted to us, destroy things we had made, and let insults fly if we did not live up to his standards that changed every day. This target was reinforced when the cops never came back to see how we were doing, and a manhunt did not ensue for the man in the woods. This target was a permanent fixture in my life. And every time satan would hit that target through the people in my life or events in my life, it simply felt like the truth. It felt so much like the truth that when people told me I was special or that they loved me or that they missed me, well, I had a hard time believing them. The target, the lie, was easier to believe. It was more real than the truth. I also had a target on me telling me I had no talents. I had nothing to offer. My life was meant for mediocrity at best because I did not do anything well. No one made a big deal out of anything I did or created. And when my teachers would praise me for my accomplishments, the target had been on my back for so long that I felt like my teachers were trying to make me feel better. It's crazy. But these are the traps that Satan uses to kill us. He may not actually kill us physically, but he can kill everything we were meant to be through making us more comfortable with his targets than God's truths. So, when the man in the woods abducts me, I will never tell because I don't matter. When my grandfather tells me I'm fat, and my older sister is the smart one, I never question it. When my mom's boyfriend keeps us up to just yell and yell at us, I don't fall apart or yell back...I'm surviving broken...the only thing holding me together by that point is a paper target fastened to my back that keeps my mouth shut and my head down. Satan is a skilled predator and he begins to line up his targets on us long before we ever realize they are there. And although they are the things that help Satan to destroy us, they are also the things we are the most comfortable with, because for most of us, they have been there for our entire life.

By the time I was in fourth grade I was exhausted and angry and smiling all the while on the outside. I remember standing in the library at our school one day with Judah. We were flipping through the card catalogue, doing some sort of assignment on how to find books using the Dewey Decimal System. I looked at Judah and said, "I think I need to go to the counselor. I think I need to talk to someone. " And she walked with me right up to Mrs. Douglas, our teacher, and told her I needed to talk to someone. And as Mrs. Douglas asked why, the tears started to fall. A million tears started falling everywhere. And I couldn't make them stop. I was shaking and sobbing. I couldn't speak. I couldn't breathe. I was so tired. I was so angry. I was so so so sad. And she walked me as fast as she could to the nurse's office. We sat there and I cried. Once it started, I couldn't make it stop. I was crying for the last five years of my life. I was crying for losing my dad and never talking to him again. I was crying for all the things my grandfather had said. I was crying for the man in the woods and all my fears and anxiety. I was crying for my sister and all she had suffered. I was crying for everything. And I thought all these tears were going to take me under. Mrs. Douglas just held me. She held me the way I had wanted to be held for years...like it was ok to fall completely apart and be 10. The counselor came in, and I cried some more. I talked about my mom's boyfriend and how much I hated him. I talked forever. I talked about my dad and missing him and not being able to understand why he didn't love us anymore. I talked about my grandfather. I talked and talked and talked. The principal called my mom. She was not happy with me about my decision to have a nervous breakdown at school. And that was the end of talking...to anyone.

That school year, Mrs. Douglas, asked Jamie, Judah, myself and a girl named Leticia to highlight books for the children in special education. We sat at a table all throughout recess. We had a huge stack of books to highlight. Green for important words. Pink for vocabulary words. Yellow for definitions. It was tedious work. And we sat inside, just the four of us, and talked and laughed. We laughed and laughed and laughed that school year and missed recess for almost the entire year. It stands out as some of the happiest moments of elementary school. Those thirty minutes inside with an important task that we had been CHOSEN to do because we were so responsible. We felt like Mrs. Douglas's favorites. We felt like we mattered. And we felt like little kids. There was no pressure to be anything else for those thirty minutes. I look back on this choice to bring these four little girls inside, away from everyone else, and give them a job. I look back and see the brilliance of a teacher who saw three broken little girls, and one little girl, Leticia, who was a Christian. Leticia invited us to church on Wednesday nights with her family. Leticia's father was finishing up his studies at UTA and she would head back to Brazil at the end of the school year. She wasn't allowed to have boyfriends. She wasn't allowed to walk home by herself. She wasn't allowed to stay up late and watch the movies we watched. And she was placed with us to laugh and bring a big dose of childhood to a table of girls who knew way too much. Mrs. Douglas was a saint. Mrs. Douglas was a brilliant saint who had no idea the impact she would have on me during recess of fourth grade by orchestrating a sanctuary in the middle of my crazy life.

We moved into a little house at the end of my fourth grade year. It was little, but it was a house. There was a washer and dryer, and we each had our own room. There was a porch swing hanging off the car port, and we could have pets so we adopted about 950 cats. There was a backyard, and we could walk to school and from school from our own house. No more staying with my grandfather before or after school. We could simply walk from our own home. I had a mirror in my room and a little sink too. My sister was so beautiful. She was tall with long legs. She had beautiful olive skin and dark brown hair, and these huge brown eyes. When I looked in the mirror, I felt like I looked disgusting. I would stand and stare in the mirror and think that my face looked deformed. No one had ever told me I was pretty. No one had ever said, "Jackie, you're pretty." And I would stand there and think how "grossed out" everyone must be when they would see me. I felt uncomfortable sometimes just talking to people because I would think they were looking at me in disgust, but I was always happy on the outside. And so much damage had been done, and my self esteem was at the bottom of a very deep barrel. I became the stereotypical abused little girl. I became promiscuous. I could never be perfect, so I could be promiscuous. By the time I was in 5th and 6th grade I was making out with boys heavily. Sometimes they were my boyfriends. Sometimes they were older than me. Sometimes we were hanging out too late with zero supervision. I liked to look the role too. I liked my jeans tight, my shirts tight. I liked short shorts and skimpy bathing suits. I felt wanted. I felt important. I felt older and responsible and pretty when boys wanted me. It was a slippery slope I was beginning to walk, and I was walking it very quickly. I look back and see how lost and lonely and desperate I was...I wanted to be loved and noticed so badly. I was willing to be loved and noticed for all the wrong reasons. I look back and I see a little girl who wanted someone to dive into the deep end and save her. And no one was diving. And no one was saving.

And then it happened. Somewhere between 5th and 6th grade my mom met Mac Martin, and someone finally dove into the water. Mac loved my mom. Mac loved my sister. And Mac loved me. And I mean, he really loved each of us. He thought I was funny. He loved to have us around. He would go out on dates with my mom and then want to talk to us too. He was this hysterical teddy bear, who I couldn't get enough hugs from. I wanted to be with him all the time. He treated me like I was a little girl. He treated me like I was the most important person to him. He wanted to go to my school programs. He wanted to know what I was up to. He hosted my 6th grade birthday party at his house. He took us shopping. He ate dinner at our house. He watched us scream and fight with each other, and he still came back. And he still loved us. I won an award that year. I won third place in a citywide competition for writing. It was the PTA Reflections contest. I was invited to a dinner for all the people who had won 3rd place and higher. He wanted to go. He also told me that I was supposed to wear a skirt. And then he had my 3rd place poem framed. He had it framed. He was proud of me. And there was not one string attached. There was not one moment when his love for us changed. And this man, this man who had never had kids, fell in love with a woman with a 12 and 13 year old daughter. This was crazy. And he just kept doing things like making the tape for the 6th grade talent show. He bought us posters for our room, came to our games, knew all our friends, and just kept coming back. He met our friend's parents, drove us to the movies, let us hang out and watch movies at his house, and made my mom laugh. And he never made her cry either, except for happy tears. And that has never changed. Mac Martin came strolling into our lives with this crazy Jesus love. He came strolling into our life with all of his goodness and all of his good upbringing and picked us. And he kept picking us over and over and over again. To this day I have no idea what made him want to step into our mess, but he stepped right in and he changed everything. To this day, Mac has never raised his voice to any of us. And man, we have deserved it. But Jesus handed us the calm in the storm. Mac was the peace that passes all understanding. And that peace moved into our home when Mac married our mom. He likes to say he married all of us. And I still like to hear him say that.

After they were married, Mac began taking us to church too. He bought my sister and I each an "Encounter" Bible for teens. It was purple with the word Encounter written in red, orange and yellow on the front. My mom handed it to me the first Sunday we went to church. I held on to it as I was ushered into a Sunday School class after the sermon. There were kids in the class I recognized from orchestra (I played the cello), but no one I knew. There was some talking. Some prayer requests (which seemed so weird to me, and I completely didn't understand). I was given a visitor card, and introduced as a visitor. Talk about summer youth camp began, and someone shared a short devotional. Then we were split into boys and girls for the lesson. I remember we sat at a rectangular table and the teacher opened up a book to begin the lesson. I have never felt that out of place in my life. There was nothing fun or funny. No one was talking to me. Everyone knew the entire routine, and I was trying to melt into the carpet. The teacher told everyone to turn to a book of their Bible, and everyone did so immediately without blinking an eye. I was floored. I was stuck. I was totally out of any sort of comfort zone, and I was the only one not knowing where that book was...I wanted to cry. But I was not a crier. So, I put my new Encounter Bible on the table, slid it over to the teacher, and said, "I do not know how to use this thing. You are going to have to help me."

I don't know who was more shocked, her or me. Clearly neither of us had been in this situation before. Clearly neither of us was prepared for that Sunday. But I think she could see on my face that I was the most lost person in the room, and had zero clue what I was doing or what to do. So, she got up, walked over to me and showed me the Table of Contents. I found my place, and she quickly realized I knew nothing. I did not know there was an Old Testament or a New Testament. I did not know any of the key players in the book either. I had heard of Jesus, and knew about the baby in the manger, Mary and Joseph, some wise men, shepherds and that was it. And where my knowledge ended her Sunday School job began, and it may have just gotten a lot harder than she ever expected. She helped me though. She answered my questions, but I didn't have many because I didn't even know what to ask. She did the best she could with this new girl. She never made me feel dumb once. And I was so thankful. This entire room was full of girls and boys with church clothes. I had never owned church clothes in my life. This entire room was full of girls and boys, who had been raised knowing everything about the Bible, and they would have jokes about little things in the Bible too...and I was the girl not having a clue what was going on. This entire room of boys and girls who prayed for poor people or "lost" kids at their school, and I didn't know what "lost" was, but I sure thought I sounded a lot more like those kids. Here I was with 400 pounds of baggage at the age of 12, making out with boys all the time, cussing like a sailor, knowing more about the world they prayed for than they ever would stuck in a room with them. They talked about being saved, and getting baptized and

I was so confused. I wanted to go back to lazy Sundays, and sleeping in, and watching TV all day. But I loved Mac, and I didn't want him to leave, so we could all just get dressed up and go to church, and wear panty hose, and if that was the only downside to Mac Martin, then I would take it.

Somewhere during that year my mom became a Christian. Somewhere during that first year of going to church, and being married to Mac, my mom joined choir and got baptized. I remember watching her up in the baptistery saying, "Jesus is Lord." This happened in front of the whole church, and after church we all stood down front and people came by and congratulated her. I had no idea why any of this happened. I did not know why or what my mom had done. I only knew that things were different. Really different. And they were changing even more. We moved to the other side of town. We moved into a big house with extra rooms. There was a park in the neighborhood, and jogging/walking trails. There were families that walked their dogs after dinner and would wave to you and say hi. There were neighborhood Christmas parties, and people who went to our church lived in the area. We got new beds. We got new furniture. We got new dishes. We had a tv room with a ping pong table. It was unbelievable. It was the best life had been ever. And Jesus was there too. Jesus was there in that Baptist church with all the Sunday School teachers who were trying to teach us about Him. Jesus was there with Mac calling us his daughters, and his family instantly introducing us the same way. Jesus was there through the good night hugs, all Mac's snoring and his infectious laughter too. Jesus came barreling into our life with Mac Martin, and dared me to believe that I was loved and wanted and that maybe some sort of good was waiting for me. And as hard as it was, there was a shred of belief. Through all the sordid mess of the last 7 years, Jesus had always sent just the right people at just the right time to hand me His hand written love letters. And here was my step dad willing to hand me the love of Jesus every single day. Every single day. And I wanted so desperately to just leave the past behind and walk into this new life. But I was broken. Really really broken. And putting me back together was going to be no easy task.

CHAPTER TWO
Near Enough

The summer before my 7th grade year, and first year of Bailey Junior High School, was the summer we moved into our new house. We moved to the complete opposite side of town. We set up our rooms, and we were allowed to decorate however we wanted. My sister and Mac painted some huge swirly colors on one of her walls, and I had posters everywhere with peace signs and a bulletin board with pictures of all of my friends. It was a great room. I had my own stereo, too, and I remember making about 900 mix tapes for all my friends or boyfriends sitting there in that room. My sister and I shared our own phone line, and there were an unbelievable number of arguments over who was supposed to be on the phone and who was waiting on a call and who had been on too long. These arguments were ridiculously loud and were pretty much a daily occurrence.

We had matching pink Conair phones. Conair, the company that made hair dryers also made phones for a while. I think we had a purple hair dryer, which was so stylish. We were able to shop at The Limited and Express and The Gap. We were able to go out to eat and go to the movies (instead of only the dollar movies). We had church clothes. We had a salon where we had our hair done. We got braces. We were planning a family vacation. We had three TVs.

It was a totally different life, and it was happier and it was way easier and it was so weird. It was weird to be around kids who had good, happy upbringings and were sheltered. I couldn't unknow the things I knew and I couldn't undo the things I had done and I couldn't erase the things that had happened to me. But we sure looked the part. We sure looked like the rest of everyone else, and in so many ways, that made my life feel like a lie.

By the time we moved into our new house, my mom was a totally different person. She had not just become a believer in Jesus, she had been radically transformed by her savior. She acted different. She dressed different. She was able to pursue her lifelong dream and become a high school history teacher. And she was an amazing teacher. She was home in the summers. She was home for dinner. She tried new recipes. She laughed more. She put her old radio in the kitchen and it was always on, and she left breakfast for us every morning. She encouraged us to get involved in school. She was excited about us going to church. She made some new friends. She tried her hand at painting. She helped with our homework. She was happy. She was different. She became the mom she had always wanted to be—she was always meant to be. She was the same person behind closed doors as she was in public. She was changed.

To this day, my mom's decision to follow Jesus stands as one of the most complete and radical transformations I have ever been witness to in my life. But I was 12, and I didn't understand how much Jesus could change someone. So, I convinced myself that she was putting on an act for my step dad. Either way, I really liked the new her. And I liked her with Mac, a lot. But when your daughter thinks you're a fraud, eventually that will not go so well for you.

That summer, my sister and I went to church camp. It was the first week school was out, and we headed out on buses to Glenrose, TX. We had invited friends to go, which made going away to camp—something I had never done before, so much easier. Everyone was given a camp T-shirt, and we all wore them on our way down to camp. It was a two-hour bus ride there, and I met some new people and mostly talked to my friend, Jamie, who I had brought with me. There were kids from all other schools, and it was actually a lot of fun from the moment we stepped onto the buses. When we got to the camp, we had to pick bunk beds in our cabin, unpack a little, go look in the mirror, and to this day I can still smell the smell of the girl's bathroom: Rave Hairspray. You could barely breathe in there. Every single girl was fixing their hair in those camp bathrooms and there was so much junior high school girl hair spray and it was Texas y'all, in the late 80's, so the hair had to be really big. It was crazy. And it was so much fun.

That year at camp was the first time I heard The Gospel. I had never heard why Jesus died on that cross. I had never heard that I could be saved. I was floored. I had never heard that I could be changed. And it sounded so good. It sounded so overwhelming. It sounded like all my sins and all my pain could be washed away. One night as the preacher was preaching and offering people the chance to follow Jesus, I walked down front. I spoke with my counselor and cried and prayed. And I felt like I could be changed. I felt like I could be different. I felt like I was loved by a carpenter king. And I wanted all of those things. I wanted them all the time. I wanted to lay all my burdens at the foot of the cross, I wanted to decide to follow Jesus and not turn back...And I could cry and love Him. And I could see how right it was for me. But I just couldn't follow Him. I could get really really near. Really near. So near to Jesus that you just might think I was a follower. But I wasn't following Him. I was still the broken girl who was not good enough and not deserving enough and who had bought too many lies in her life to believe that things could change. But I could talk the talk, and sometimes that seems to be all that matters.

People were so excited that I had gone down front. And so was I, really. I really was excited that I was going to start over in this new house with a new church and this new, awesome Jesus. I went to a ton of church events that summer. And I met fabulous people. People really tried to reach out to me. It was genuine. But I always felt like the girl from the other side of the universe, who messed around with boys, cussed, and wore the wrong clothes. I didn't know any of the songs they sang about the Bible. I didn't know any of the Old Testament stories they had learned growing up in VBS; so there was this great divide. The target was already on me telling me I did not matter and I had nothing to offer, so I worked hard to understand sometimes and other times I just came to church to flirt and meet boys or simply because I had to go to church. Sometimes I would answer questions honestly in Sunday School and know that no one knew what to say to me. Sometimes I would hear other kids give the perfect answers, and I would despise them. Sometimes I wished that I were different. And sometimes I wished everyone else were more like me. Still, most days I felt as if I stuck out like a sore thumb, with a scarlet letter tattooed somewhere on my forehead telling other church going kids that I was not like them at all. I was wild.

I had fun that summer in lots of ways. I had fun with all of the events at church, but really only when I brought my own friends because I still didn't fit with the other kids. I had fun going swimming with Jamie and Judah at the university pool and having crushes on boys way older than us. I had fun lying about my age when we were out and giving boys my number, because they thought I was in high school. But I was so self-conscious about my face. I was so self-conscious about the way my face looked it is hard to explain. At times I felt like the boy in the movie, "Mask," with Cher. I began to feel like my face looked horrifying and the only good thing I had to offer was my winning personality and over developed body. Low self esteem coupled with childhood abuse and throw in a dose of looking way older, and the slippery slope I had begun to walk was only getting more slippery.

Sometimes I would cry because of how ugly I felt. Sometimes people accidentally confirmed it by telling me how gorgeous my older sister was, and how we looked nothing alike. It made it so much worse. But I was an amazing and skilled actress. I could fake confidence better than anyone, and I was funny, which was an enormous bonus for me. You would have to spend loads and loads of time with me to figure out how low my self-esteem was, because I was pretty much bent on making everyone think I did not care about their opinions. The act worked all through school, but underneath it all was that little 6-year-old girl I was desperately trying to suffocate while she stood frozen somewhere in the woods.

By the time school started and I was officially a junior high student, I had my feet firmly planted in two worlds. I had my church world, filled with Sunday school, lock ins and lock outs, convicting conversations and notes passed in church; and I had my "real" life, too, filled with my sweet, seventh grade boyfriend, who I messed around with way more than any other church girl, and sneaking out and the beginnings of making some pretty horrible choices. Sometimes I could feel how much the girls at my church talked about me. Sometimes I could feel how fake they were when they asked me questions they knew the answers to...it wasn't all of the girls, but it seemed the most "popular" church girls could be the meanest about you behind your back. I felt sorry for them because their lives seemed so boring and filled with trivial problems, and at the same time I felt sorry for me because I could not adapt to a life of having trivial problems at all.

As much as I was trying to be friends with all the right people and all the "good" kids at school, I was still utterly drawn to all the "bad" kids because they just seemed real and they just accepted you right where you were. There were always exceptions to the people at church...always. However, I constantly felt the stares and whispers from kids and parents alike. I did not fit, and I pretty much knew it. There were long conversations with Judah and Jamie about how we just didn't fit. We were in athletics at school, in honors classes, made good grades and yet we were not like other kids, because we knew too much. When you have seen "too much" long before seventh grade, you can't worry about what lip-gloss to buy. You can try to care, but you care more about the kid in your class with their head down every day, who gets in trouble every time class convenes. You identify more with them because at least they are being honest about how they feel, at least they don't fake their pain away. And you worry about those kids. You're trying out for volleyball and basketball, playing your cello, and going to the mall—trying to forget how different you are—and they are embracing it. I felt like a liar around those kids.

I had one teacher in particular that served as the voice of Jesus that year of 7th grade. She was my history teacher, and quite honestly I can't remember at all which history she taught—US or Texas or World. Her class was not riveting, but I liked her. She was older. She was a grandmother's age. She was not hip or cool. Her hair was way out of style, and she was not particularly tolerant; but I really liked her. I cannot tell you what it was, but there was a connection there, and I looked forward to her class every day. Sometimes we were allowed to give our opinion on different political topics. (Maybe this is why I liked her class so much.) It was a time when we had the opportunity to say what we thought.

One day I was standing on a soapbox, making a point. It was a point about the underdogs, kids who were poor who deserved a shot, and I was feeling pretty intensely about it. I was talking loud and hammering my point home. When I was finished the class was silent, and I was totally embarrassed. Mrs. Lee turned to the class and said, "Class, remember the name Jackie Wildman. She is going to be a force to be reckoned with some day." And for one instant, one tiny moment, I believed her. For a second I bought it and thought maybe I could run for public office or tell people they were not forgotten or write about things that mattered to me. And then I could feel the targets (because more were always added) on my back, and I remembered that I was not smart and I had nothing to offer and I didn't really matter to anyone and this teacher was just saying this to make me feel better since I had made a fool of myself in her class. But Jesus didn't let it go. And if I tried to remain silent in her class and do less than offer my opinion or my outlook on a situation, Mrs. Lee would simply say that they class needed to know what I thought. Her encouragement was more than just a teacher encouraging a student. She began to hand me my voice daily. And by the end of that year, she had made the journey, totally unbeknownst to her, to visit a very sad and lonely place inside my heart and offer a little healing.

That same year, at Christmas time, Jeannie and I called my dad's mom, GrandMary, to wish her a Merry Christmas. We did this every year. We called and had a somewhat awkward conversation with a lady we hadn't seen in years who could barely hear, but she worked so hard to hear us in those conversations. It was precious to me even when I was thirteen and a total jerk at times. She asked us to call early that year. When we did, my step mom, Maureen, answered. Shocked, my sister instantly hung up the phone. If Maureen was there, then our dad for sure was there. And what if we could talk to him? Jeannie and I were sitting in her room, and we didn't know what to do. She called back, and you could have heard a pin drop— two girls holding their breath, waiting to see if they could talk to their dad whom they hadn't spoken to since they were very little.

The thought that he wouldn't want to talk to us was terrifying, but the thought that he would want to talk to us was terrifying too. It was such a surreal moment, and when we finally talked to him and he so desperately wanted to talk to us—there were so many emotions that night. I don't have any clue what he said or what we talked about. I knew that I was so afraid to let the phone conversation end because what if that was it? What if we could say we loved each other and my dad cried and then that was it? What would happen then? Would we just tell everyone that this one time we talked to our dad on the phone? He wanted to come see us, and we wanted him to come see us. And it was crazy.

When we finally got off the phone and went and told our mom exactly who we had been talking to on the phone, she looked like she was going to pass out. She sat down and cried. I walked around the corner to my friend's house where other kids were watching a movie. I told all of them I talked to my dad and I hadn't talked to him in like eight years. I remember my friend's parents being really worried about me and asking if I was ok a bunch. I kept getting all choked up. And I kept telling everyone he seemed so nice and that I had a little sister. And he wanted to see us. And he said he loved us. And that part felt so weird to me. How could he love us? He did not even know us; even the people who did know us didn't necessarily love us. And then there was the issue with my mom. She was finally happy, and if we went and met our dad and he was kind and we liked him then how much would she fall apart? And I couldn't let that happen. She was just getting pieced back together.

As excited as I was about my dad, I was so dang skeptical. I was living life the way it had always been lived, which meant that getting my hopes up was the dumbest thing ever because adults said whatever they wanted just to make themselves feel better—and how could he mean he loved us? I would not fully understand this until the moment I met my son, Jacob, almost fifteen years later. From the moment I lay eyes on that baby boy, I loved him with my whole life. If he had left my arms at nine minutes old and I didn't see him for the next twenty years, I would remember everything about those first nine minutes and every detail of his little face until I died. My dad was not a liar, but I could just not understand that kind of unconditional love without any boundaries at all. But my dad could, and that is the beautiful thing about when Jesus wants you to know you're loved: he sends a person into your life who loves enormously. Enormously.

My dad came and visited us. I think he went to one of my orchestra concerts. It was awkward— awkward with my mom being there, but it was good, and Mac was so great about everything. Mac made it easier. Mac loved as big as my dad, Kent, loved. If someone loved his girls then that seemed important, especially if it was their father. And vice versa. But it was not in any way a happy ending where there were family vacations together and Christmas cards in the mail. But I sure wish it had been that way.

We would go visit Nashville that summer. I was nervous and excited and so nervous and so worried about my mom. I was worried it would be horrible; I was worried it would be great. Either one seemed like a nightmare for me. If it was horrible, my mom for sure would come unglued and find a way to make my dad's life miserable. If it was great, my mom would for sure come unglued and just be so sad and feel like she was losing us. It felt like a lose/lose situation. But we got on a plane and we went to see my dad, my step mom, and meet my little sister, Dycee, for the first time. We had not been back to Nashville since Halloween of 1980 and there were people and places still trapped in my memories. And there was a part of me that needed to see these people and these places and know that they really existed. I needed to know that this time period really existed. I needed to know that the itty-bitty girl in the pictures laughing was me and other people remembered that me. And I was going to see the people who knew me as a happy little me.

It ended up being wonderful in Nashville. I ended up having the cutest little sister ever. She was gorgeous and funny and creative and so loved. And my dad and Maureen, my step mom, were doing a really good job raising her too. And they lived in this awesome house. It was big and spacious with windows on the front and back from floor to ceiling. It was in a wooded area outside of Nashville, so sometimes you could see deer in the backyard. There were long, creative, intellectual conversations to be had at the kitchen table. They took us shopping for the artwork for our bedroom. There was different food than I had ever eaten in my life (my step mom was healthy before being healthy was cool). It was a slower pace. It was a different world. And it was good. And I felt calm there. But inside all of that goodness was so much pain because my dad had been living here in this calm and peaceful world for so long and, well, I wasn't there. I wasn't calm and peaceful and my heart was a little broken. But I was never one to have those tough conversations or cry, so I just said everything was great and that I loved everyone. And I did. I really did. But I wondered how and why everyone in my entire universe could forget about me so easily. And I remembered the target I wore everywhere I went. I didn't really have much to offer, and no one really cared about me anyway. Oh, the lies we listen to all day long when we are not willing to say them out loud. If I, at any moment, had said any of this out loud, maybe some healing could have taken place. But silence always felt like my friend, even though I talked all the time.

We went back home after a couple of weeks, and I began to fall apart at the end of that summer. Not in tears or nervous breakdowns; I just bought in to all the lies in my head. I was finished being good. I was finished trying. I was finished playing games, so I did what so many children do when their lives are filled with their own personal unexplained and never talked about tragedy: I started to split. I would be good in the right places to be good, and I would be so bad in every other place.

I started smoking the summer before eighth grade. I also had a new boyfriend who was actually my age. He was a really nice guy, but we were so overly promiscuous. I had sex for the first time that fall, and I was only 13 years old. I didn't think a thing about it either. I didn't care who knew. I didn't care what other people thought. I didn't feel thirteen. I didn't look thirteen. And I certainly had not lived the life of most 13 year olds. My best friends were not shocked, and no one seemed worried about my decision.

When I look back on that girl, when I see her total apathy for who she was, I see her. Somewhere inside of her was a little girl. Somewhere inside of her was a little girl that had not been happy in years and knew no peace. Somewhere inside of her was a little girl who had gotten so close to Jesus but could not commit to that type of love, because that type of love was meant for little girls who were worth something. It was not all my "poor choices" that were holding me back from all of Jesus. It was simply that I did not care what happened to me anymore. I didn't care one bit. And this was about to spiral out of control.

By ninth grade, I had broken up with my nice boyfriend and moved on. I was dating older guys. I was going to clubs. I was sneaking out on weeknights and sleeping through school. I had friends who were drug dealers. I had friends who stole cars. I had friends who did not even live with their parents. My grades went from A's and B's to barely hanging on. I failed classes. I cussed out my mom and my step dad. I drank and smoked all the time. I was only in ninth grade and I was dating guys in college. I had dropped out of orchestra. I hadn't made cheerleader with the rest of my friends. I had nothing to really hold on to. I had such a bad reputation that walking into church I felt like I was going to catch on fire. And I always smelled like a chimney, so I wonder what the Sunday School teachers thought of the little girl who wreaked of cigarettes. But no one ever said anything to me. No one ever called me to the carpet or was able to stop me from doing anything I was doing. I was still good at smiling at family functions. I was still great at talking to adults and making them like me. I was still great at just enough so that you couldn't worry too much at me. There were some people in my youth group who were much older who truly tried to reach out to me and Judah and Jamie and they could call our bluff every once in awhile and maybe I felt guilty here and there, but to be honest, I was having way too much bad girl fun to stop and try to be a goody two shoes. Girls who were goody goodies really wanted to be bad like me. Or at least I told myself they did. And girls like me, we were meant to be really really bad.

The very end of the summer before my sophomore year of high school, I was at my worst. I fought with my mom all the time. If my mom tried to ground me or make me stay home, I would call someone I knew who drove and have them come pick me up. I was headed to high school, and I was hanging out with way older people, and I didn't even bother going to church much anymore. So many times when I went I was still drunk from the night before. I remember standing, praying, and swaying some Sundays with Judah beside me, laughing through the whole prayer because we could barely stand up and sleeping through the whole sermon. My mom and step dad were important in our church and everyone knew them. I wonder how much they dreaded me during this time in my life. But Jesus gave me people who had this crazy unconditional quality to them when it came to loving me: my step dad, my dad, my step mom, and my mom—my mom. She had become one of those crazy loving and forgiving type people after she found Jesus. He really is that big, y'all.

But I was determined to make a mess of it all. The last month of summer, I started hanging out with two guys in my grade who did not go to school. They were hanging out with two guys in their late twenties. I look back on this and see there are no two guys who are almost thirty who hang out with fourteen year old kids. These were bad, bad, bad men. We went to Taco Bell with them one afternoon and then went back to their apartment. We started drinking early. My parents had no idea where I was. I tried to get some girl to tell my parents I was at her house, but I could barely make sense by the time I remembered it was time to cover my own tracks. People were doing drugs. I was going in and out of consciousness. Around 3 AM, my mom and step dad had figured out where we were. We hid in the closet of these guys' apartment and they lied and fought with my parents, not telling them Judah and I were hiding and smoking in their closet. I remember cracking up because we burned a hole in some of the clothes as my mom was desperate outside the door. By the time someone drove me home the next day, I had made about 982,000 poor choices and was certain there was nothing left to go home to. I sat at our kitchen table, and nothing was said except that I was grounded for the rest of the summer. And I was only allowed to go to church functions. And I could deal with that. I was tired, and sometime while sleeping on a bathroom floor the night before, I began to feel like this was enough and I was tired of being this bad. Let me just say that inside of every "bad" kid there is a little kid who has been hurt.

Any girl who sleeps around at the age of fourteen has abuse in her past. Any kid that is drinking and smoking heavily by the age of fourteen has severe self-esteem issues and is hurting. And Jesus loves them. He loves them so much. And He truly wants them to know that as soon as possible. He doesn't look at them and feel disgusted. He looks at them and wants to take all the targets off their back and hold them and tell them He was there all the days their world seemed to fall apart. And He desperately needs strong adults to step in with 450 pounds of love and save some beautiful kiddos laying injured on the battlefield. Jesus wants their lives to be different. He did not create me or them or any of us with a million pounds of baggage to be what our targets, Satan's lies, say that we are.

I started at Arlington High School with one goal in mind: I was going to be good. I was sad. I was repentant, and I was ready for anything other than the constant train wreck I had been on for the past couple of years. My mom and Mac didn't trust me a bit, and I totally understood why, so when they didn't let me do things, I said ok. I quit hanging out with my "old" friends and started trying to hang out with the good girls. I tried to have a good boyfriend too. And it was working. I was going to the movies. I was going to school functions. I had made some fantastic friends in my youth group at church. I was at church all the time, and I had chosen the role of bad-girl-gone-good. It was a fantastic role, but something wasn't right. I was trying to be someone else. How could I find a place for the real me that Jesus would actually love? The fact was, all these things that had happened to me or I had done were real and they were part of my story, but embracing it was too hard. And being shallow was killing me. And I had this all wrapped up in Jesus, and I look back now and wonder how much He wanted to tell me to stop trying so hard and just let Him love me. But I was working hard to be worth something. I was working hard to prove every bad person in my life wrong and show everyone who had talked bad about me how good I could be. This momentary transformation would last for a few years, but it couldn't be the lasting substitute for allowing Jesus to just love me and teach me follow Him into His plan for my life.

During my sophomore year, I quit going to Sunday School and began teaching and serving at Mission Arlington. I taught Sunday School each Sunday morning to a group of elementary-aged girls living in low-income apartments. They were allowed to go, each Sunday, to church in an apartment Mission Arlington rented for this sole purpose. There were other teachers too and we sang songs and held church on the poor side of town with a bunch of kids, whose parents we never even saw. I felt right at home. I knew these little girls. I knew their life stories. I knew they knew way too much by the second grade and parking lots were their playgrounds with kids of all ages. I knew what the future held for them, too, if someone didn't step into their life. And I loved them so much.

I loved preparing for the lesson every Sunday morning, and I loved doing something real for Jesus. I loved doing what Jesus would do...He would go to the people who needed Him most and love them and feed them (we always brought food) and tell them that they were special and tell them that He saw them right where they were. It was life changing for me to go and be uncomfortable a bit and have meaningful conversations with people I barely knew—holding kiddos when they cried, praying for them. It was beautiful. It would stay tucked into my heart for the rest of my life.

I ended up teaching that Sunday morning Bible study for three years. Sitting on the floor of an empty apartment and teaching the girls from the little worksheets I had printed off, trying to answer questions, and trying to end the constant argument of who was allowed to sit in my lap was the first time in my life that I had felt useful. And being useful was amazing.

But I still didn't have a personal relationship with Jesus. I had become a good person, and I could get really near to Jesus any time. And if someone wanted to talk about Jesus and read a verse, I could tell them what I thought it meant. But I did not know Him at all. I did not know anything He said during His ministry. I did not know what He had done when He lived here on earth. I knew He saved people and healed people, but this is where my knowledge ended. People would still talk about people from the New or Old Testament and I was completely clueless. I liked being good. I liked being kind. I wanted people to come to church. I wanted people to become better. And all of that was wrapped up in Jesus, so it appeared that I was the best of the best, this bad girl who had turned her life around. But I had done it through my own will, and I had felt bad and I had felt sorry for the things I had done. I could talk the talk, but I could not give Jesus my heart or my life, because deep down inside I knew who I was: I was cold and bad. I was the girl who left her sister behind in the woods—and this was all an act anyway. I could never be good enough. I could just say all the right words. Words were my friend. I had spent my life playing games; I could play this game too. It just had different rules and different results, but I could play. And I loved this game. I mean, I won camper of the year at camp that summer. But deep down inside, I knew (because the targets had been placed on my back so long ago) exactly who I was.

My junior year of high school was probably the best year of school for me. I loved my honors English teacher, Dr. Clark. Judah and I were in this awesome Bible Study together. The youth intern had paired us (two bad girls gone good who still smoked a pack of cigarettes a day) with two boys who had never made a poor choice in their lives. When we met, one night a week at the youth intern's house, we had some of the best discussions ever. I think we all opened each other's eyes to other people. I think we saw inside the life of people who were totally different than us, and it was incredible. We found out how alike we all were, even with all of our differences. Jesus reached into that room once a week and spoke precious words into my ears of how much He loved me and how much I was just a normal girl who had lived in abnormal circumstances and been asked to make extraordinarily difficult choices at way too young an age. He did unbelievable work in my life that year, and I was getting close to following Him for real.

The youth intern called my bluff one night and asked when I was going to tell someone that I had been abused. I asked what he was talking about, and he said that it was so obvious how broken I was. I cried on the front porch of the intern house for a long time.

I had a wonderful boyfriend that year who went to Young Life and prayed with me and would come to church with me. I have about 9 million pictures of us together at church camp and Wednesday night church and out on dates. It was the first time I had cared deeply for a boy. He was so good. He was so on the "right" track. He took me on dates, and we hung out with all his friends and my friends and it was so good and so happy. I loved his parents. I loved his sister. I loved everything I could see my life being if we got married—I could make good choices and he would make good choices and we would make big dinners and have silly kids and life would be perfect. But we were in high school and he was going away to college. The bottom line was I needed him to make me better and he did not need me at all. The summer before my senior year, his friend told me he had been cheating on me the entire time we were dating, and my heart broke into hundreds of little pieces. And with that, The Enemy reconfirmed what he had been telling me all along: I was not worth anything, I did not have anything to offer, and I was a bad girl who could never be good. The signs that had been strategically placed on my back my whole life began to tug at my heart, and I started to unravel little by little.

That same summer, a group of guys would get kicked out of church camp for all the stuff they were doing while they were there. I was floored. Why would you kick out the kids who needed to be there the most? When this whole chunk of guys left, my heart hurt. And then that September of my Senior year of high school, the youth intern called a meeting. This was a man who had taken time with me. This was a man who had called my bluff and saw the "me" inside the game. This was a man who didn't want anything more for me than to know Jesus. He stood in front of all the parents and said he had been lying. He was not in seminary. He had been going to the movies a lot and not going to classes. He was asked to leave the church and a new youth minister was hired. I was floored and hurt and confused. If even the Jesus people would lie, then this was getting pointless. Finally, the team I worked with at Mission Arlington was excited it was summer. They were hoping "to get some baptisms" that summer. I should have asked them what they meant. I should have said that their words made me think they were working toward a quota. Instead, I said nothing and just never came back and never answered their phone calls. Jeannie was away at college and life was just different. I was finished. It was over. I was done with all these crazy people who said they were good then lied and who didn't care about me in the first place and who only cared about rules and baptisms and looking good.

My senior year of high school, I just walked away. I walked away from church. I walked away from being good. I walked away from caring about other people. I walked away from wanting to ever get married. I walked away from the little six-year-old girl left standing in the woods. I walked away from all my pain, and I became angry instead. Angry was working for me, and not caring was working even more. I was fun and funny; I could take you or leave you, and I didn't think too much about that either.

Throughout high school I would visit my dad and family in Nashville once or twice a year, but that began to feel like a lie too. They didn't know much about my day-to-day, and I didn't have to tell them, so when I was there I would feel fake. And that was not going to work for me. I saw my dad and step mom and younger sister less and less, until I barely saw them or talked to them at all. My relationship was good with my mom and step dad because I was willing to lie to them about everything. The only person who knew the entire truth of my life was Judah. She was the only one who knew it all from day one. And Jesus is kind and gracious. And He gave me one person to walk my truth out with so that one person could completely understand me. And I had at least one place to be myself and one person who knew that I was just walking a really long road. And Jesus knew too. He knew, every moment I walked further away from truly knowing Him, to send just the right person with just the right words at just the right time.

Mac's dad, Papaw, was one of those people. He just always loved me. He always made me laugh. He always enjoyed having me around. He encouraged me to go to college. When my mom applied for me to go to school at the University of North Texas, I was floored at my acceptance. And I decided to go. And my grandfather was so excited that I was going to his alma mater. He was excited, and that was so priceless to me. He was proud of me. He gave me the last little jolt of love I needed to make a few things happen. I would go to school. I would live in the dorms. I would do something with my life. I wanted to be a writer or a teacher or a counselor. Maybe I could help people. Maybe there was hope for me yet. And my grandfather was there at my graduation party. My grandfather was there for so many milestones, and he wasn't even my "real" grandfather, but he seemed to love me so much. He seemed to think that I was special. And I thought he was so special. I thought he was one of the neatest people I had ever met. And Jesus loved me through him those last few months before I would leave Arlington, TX.

Jesus laid some foundations that were real, and there were moments when I knew there was more to this whole Jesus thing than just being good. But I wasn't willing to pursue that too much longer. I hadn't gone to a church function in over a year. I hadn't done much of anything near Jesus for awhile, and I was ok with it. But Jesus was not ok with it at all. And He never gave up. And He never quit putting people in my path to pull the little girl out of the woods, out of her grandfather's house, out of the way of her mother's boyfriend, and out of the arms of all the wrong guys and into His.

CHAPTER THREE

Front Porch Jesus

College for me looked similar to what it did for most people on the outside. There were lots of parties. There were things that only happen in college—staying out until the sun came up, eating at restaurants with crazy names, knowing people who you would never bump into in regular life. I cut ties with high school. I cut ties as fast as I could. I was going to be someone different. I was going to be a better me.

I joined a sorority, and shortly thereafter began to end my friendship with Judah. I still cannot understand at all why I made that choice, but I was pretty sure I would be on to a new life at any given moment. And I couldn't have any trappings from the past. I had to move forward and be someone new. I had to leave it all behind. I went to college with my boyfriend from my senior year of high school, and by the end of my freshman year of college that relationship had ended. What was a single girl to do in college? I look back and I see Jesus crazy at work during the beginning of my freshman year. He put people in my dorm who would repeatedly invite me to Bible Study or church. These were people who would talk to me about the gospel and how much Jesus loved me, and I just got annoyed. He placed a guy in one of my classes, named Ben, who had a frank and honest conversation with me one day outside class about how I was pretty, but he could not date a girl like me who was not a Christian. He placed good people in my life. He placed

Judah at the same college too—someone who knew who I was, and I walked away from it all.

I made new friends. I made friendships that I thought would last a lifetime my freshman year. I made friends that I spent every day with, and we were inseparable. I could share pieces of my life with them, but I couldn't share all of my life. I could tell them how I used to be really poor and I could tell them that I used to not have any dreams of going to college and I could tell them that my stepdad changed my life, but I could not tell them any of my real problems. I could not tell them the images that woke me up at night or the things that made me super nervous or how I was losing a battle on the inside more and more every day.

I ended up living with my "new best friend" and her boyfriend in an apartment. It was not a good situation. I was spiraling out of control quickly by my sophomore year. I was sleeping with everyone. I was keeping my feet firmly placed in two worlds: my new world being in a sorority, where I held offices and went to mixers, and a whole new world with 500 pounds of freedom and no one looking over my shoulder. I could do whatever I wanted whenever I wanted, and sometimes I did just that. I made a whore of myself. I spent time with other girls who lived in two worlds, and at some point during my sophomore year there was the biggest, most painful falling out. My new friends were not my friends. And I had never experienced anything like the viciousness of girls tearing girls apart. It was horrible. It still makes me cringe to think about it. But God is good and gracious, and through this falling out and world falling apart feeling, I became friends with different girls in my sorority. And that part of my life felt happy and calm for the most part.

I could tell you a million things wrong with being in a sorority. But for me, it was a place where I was ok. My sophomore year, Jesus handed me a group of friends who would stand by me through thick and thin. They were kinder. They were funnier. They teased me about being their wilder friend. There was way too much singing when we were together. They knew my mom and stepdad and adored them. This part of my life was really happy. We took classes together sometimes. We met for lunch and laughed and laughed. And they were all just good people. And I could tell them a million things, but I could never tell them about the real me. I couldn't tell them how much I hated myself for always living in two worlds. I couldn't tell them how much I wanted to be like them and be happy and make good choices. So, I just continued to sleep around, and I went home with more guys than I care to remember. Some of them were regular hook ups, few I actually dated, some were just friends with benefits, but any way you sliced it sex clearly had no meaning to me.

And I was friends, good friends, with really great girls who were waiting till they got married to have sex. And I was a friend of girls who would never sleep around. And I was the girl getting carried out of bars—wild and crazy and so unhappy on the inside. Why they were friends with me I will never know, but I believe it was Jesus' way of keeping me from diving headlong into a pit of sex and drugs. He gave me this group of girls who just loved me, and that kind of love is the kind of love Jesus can completely use to hold His wounded children close to Him.

And then there was Judah. When people who knew the other side of my life began to bash me, the girl who I had dismissed once I pledged a sorority, she stood up for me. She stood up for me. And through some pain and well-deserved heartache, Jesus reminded me that He had chosen for me a constant companion to live life with and that was Judah. He gave me a person who always knew everything about me. For someone who typically hid one life from the other, having a person who genuinely loved you despite your crazy secrets would play out again and again in my life as a gift that Jesus gave special to me.

So, I could tell you stories about the girl I was. I could tell you that I slept with a guy regularly who would never even hold my hand in public. I could tell you I slept with people that disgusted me. I could tell you that people cheated on their long term girlfriends with me. I could tell you that I woke up sometimes and wondered how I had ended up where I was and had no clue who I was with. I can tell you that people took utter advantage of me. I can tell you that one night I was really high in some house somewhere in Denton and the guy I was with overdosed on cocaine and I did nothing. I didn't call 911. I didn't wake anyone in the house up. I just sat there as his face turned blue and blood was coming out of his mouth and nose and hoped that he would not die. And he didn't die. And he didn't quit using and I kept hanging out with him anyways. I can tell you I had a reputation a million miles long. I can tell you I deserved every sentence whispered about me. I can tell you that I had my friends that I got stoned with and tripped mushrooms with and hung out barefoot with, and I had another group of friends who I wore matching shirts with and sang sorority songs with and was a good daughter with. And I can tell you that somewhere in between my two worlds was me. Somewhere in between the "good girl" and the "bad girl" or the "hippy girl" and the "preppy girl" or the "smart girl" and the "life is a party girl" was me with my life divided in two by my own doing, and my head was spinning all the time.

There was so much damage done to my self-esteem by sleeping around. Girls can tell you a million things about this. They can tell you that it's no big deal and everyone has to have a little fun, but feeling used and unloved wears on you. It wears on you being the girl whose phone is going crazy at 2 AM when the bars close, but never has a date...ever.

During my crazy college life, I had a neighbor who went to church and was involved in a church group too. He was super funny, and so good looking, and we hung out all the time. We would laugh and laugh together, but he would never date me. He was looking for a girl who was a Christian. He had no interest in a girl who he had seen come in and out of her apartment throwing up, being carried, or with a steady stream of guys who didn't seemed to come back much.

One night we were sitting outside on my porch, and he said to me, "Someday these guys are going to be really sad they missed out on you." I was really surprised he even thought this, and he went on to say, "Someday you will get your life together, and you are smart and funny and pretty and you will make someone really happy." I cried in my room that night for a million reasons. I wished he would step in and make my life better. I wished that "someday when I would get my life together" was now. I wished that I believed that someday I would make someone very happy, because it didn't seem like that would ever be in the cards for a girl like me. But I loved that he was my neighbor, and I loved that there was someone who really saw me, in spite of all the things I did to make myself go away.

And I started to become angry in college. I remember sitting in an Abnormal Psych class one semester and the professor describing what happens to families riddled by alcoholism. He was describing the long-term effects on children of alcoholics, and I saw my whole family in his description. And all of a sudden, it occurred to me that my grandfather had been drunk when I was little. All those times of yelling and getting a 5-year-old to take puffs on his cigarettes, and sleeping the morning away...he was drunk or hungover. I was so angry that no one had passed on this knowledge to me. I was angry that I had gone years thinking I was the most stupid and annoying kid in the universe. I was angry that I was left in his care. And I began to look at other pieces of my life and really dig into them.

I had a fairly strong relationship with my dad and stepmom when I was in college. They were so kind and loving. They had raised this really great daughter, Dycee, who was creative and engaging and was doing amazing things even though she was just a kid. And my dad was always so supportive of me and interested in me and loved talking to me when I would see him. And he was supposed to be the bad guy. I started asking him why he never tried to get in touch with us. Why he never helped my mom out with money, and when I found out that he had tried—he had tried to call us, tried to send money, sent presents, and tried to be a part of our life—I was furious. How could anyone allow their children to think that they were unwanted? The damage this had done to my self-esteem was tremendous. The amount of time that I grew up feeling unloved and unwanted could have been lessened. And here were the results. Here I stood hoping that someday some guy would love me enough to look past all the crap to see that I really was a nice person. And with just a few key pieces of information I might have felt better? My world was rocking. My world was crashing down.

The angrier I became the more I hated Jesus. There are people in the world who are atheists, and they are atheists. They don't care that you don't agree with them, and they are not worried about what you believe. They know what they believe or don't believe and they are just fine. Then there are the angry atheists. I was one of those. I was angry with a God who I swore up and down did not exist. I was angry with people who believed in Him. And I thought the people who believed in Jesus were some of the dumbest, most clearly brainwashed people I had ever seen. I used to love when students from a nearby church would come to campus and try to evangelize people. It was one of my favorite pastimes to confuse the Christians or make them question their own theology. I read books disproving Christianity, and I went to psychics to find the path I was supposed to be following. I believed anything and everything, and I was ok with denouncing Jesus and thinking I had been stupid to ever consider Him in the first place. It was a low time for me.

And then my grandfather died. Pawpaw.

He had a stroke. One day he was fine and the next day he had a stroke. He hung on for a few days, and I went to see him before he died. I drove like crazy as fast as I could to Arlington to stand at the bedside of an old man who had loved me like a grandfather should love a granddaughter. I stood by his bed and remembered that we were the kids who he knew all about. He had seen us running up and down the street his and my grandmother's art gallery was on long before my mom had married Mac. He knew that my friends' parents were the people who were trying to steal water from his art studio since there's had been cut off, and he had kindly walked over to his neighbors and bought their house. He had been superintendent of Arlington ISD for over two decades and knew everyone. People loved to hear him give speeches...he made you laugh and cry all at once. And as I stood there next to his bed, I realized how much I not only loved this old man but I respected him. I respected everything he stood for, and he stood for a lot. He was a servant leader. He believed the greatest way to lead was to serve. And I knew he had served and loved two little girls from the wrong side of town in a way that was above and beyond what most "step-grandparents" ever do, and his love helped to change and shape my life.

While I stood there looking at the kindest old man who was larger than life, he opened his eyes and said through the speech that comes only after a stroke, "What are you doing here? You go back to school." And I told him I loved him. And he smiled and patted my hand.

So, I drove back to school. And when he died later that night, I cried and cried. I went to the funeral not long after. I sat with my mom and Mac, and PawPaw's sisters were there— these little old ladies from Josephine, TX. They were country. And I was taken aback by how they all remembered my name. I was sitting at a funeral of a man I loved dearly, and dumbfounded by the fact that not just my grandfather but his sisters had also welcomed us in to their family. They had bought Jeannie and I Christmas presents that first Christmas after my mom and Mac were married. They were excited to meet us. This legacy of love ran deep in my step-dad's family. It had been handed down. They were loving. And my grandfather's love had filled a church sanctuary to the brim. His was a life lived and loved well for Jesus. Everyone who spoke told funny stories and sweet stories and talked about his love for Jesus. And his children, grandchildren, and wife were experiencing the enormous hole his absence would leave. And I thought for the whole entire funeral how I wanted to live a life like his: big and meaningful—the type that would fill a sanctuary with people who loved me. And I saw people that day I hadn't seen in years. I saw people who had loved me and tried to reach out to me, people who wondered if I had found a good church home in Denton, TX, people who had seen a glimpse of who I could be when I was near enough to Jesus. Part of me wanted to get in my car and get out of town instantly; part of me wanted to stay forever.

But it was my senior year of school, and I went back with all my sadness and all my anger. I had begun to rebuild my relationship with my dad and my step mom and younger sister, Dycee, while I was in the end of college. That part of my life was good. That part of my life I wasn't angry at just yet. And Mac, I could never be angry at Mac. But everyone else I could find reasons to question everything about them and everything they had done or not done for me. Honestly, I look back and see how I was walking through the stages of grief. I just got stuck in anger for a long, long time.

I would start dating my husband that Christmas. I was home from college, and he was home from the Navy. We had grown up together. I met him when I was seven and he was eight at a YMCA summer camp. Corey had been in my life for as long as I could remember. Not really a huge part of my life but on the outskirts. When my mom married Mac, we sat behind another family at church that Mac's family had set behind for decades. Corey and I were the step kids in these two families.

We were in orchestra together in Junior High School. I played the cello and he played the second violin. I only remember him spending the majority of his time in On Campus Suspension. In high school if he was at church, he typically wanted to know where my older sister was, or we might pass stupid notes during the sermon. But nothing huge. He asked me out once, and I reminded him that he was engaged. Corey, when we started dating, was getting divorced from his high school girlfriend. They had married while he was in the Navy and things had not worked out. His brother had died that same year. Corey was sad. I was sad. Corey and I were cut from the same cloth in many ways, and we were two broken people trying to overcome the odds that had been stacked against us since we were little kids.

And I felt comfortable with him. I felt like I could breathe in and out with him. I didn't feel judged. He didn't care that I had just spent the last four years being extraordinarily wild because he had been really wild too. He didn't care that I was angry. He was angry too. He didn't mind that my family had so many hurdles and dysfunctions to it. His family did too. We also both had walked away from Jesus. Corey had gone to church his entire life. He had gone to children's camp and youth camp. He had gone to weekly church choir and Sunday School. But the whole relationship with Jesus—I heard him explain it to my son's once, and he said, "I could not see Jesus anywhere. There was no one in my life that I could see who was following Jesus and whose life was different because of Jesus, outside of going to church." So he just went with the flow until he was old enough to not go at all. Corey wasn't angry at a God he didn't believe in. He was just angry and sad. But when we were together we laughed and had fun and he seemed to cherish me.

And maybe for once everything was going to just be different. We were engaged within three months.

We had a whirlwind romance, and when I finished my coursework at the end of July, I moved to Virginia to be with him. It was the craziest thing I had ever done, really. It made no sense at all to move for a guy who I had dated while we were home for Christmas, which all in all added up to be thirteen days. We had flown back and forth across the country to see each other. And so, I packed up my little efficiency apartment into a UHaul, Corey flew into town, and we drove to Virginia Beach, Virginia. The drive itself was crazy. We stopped along the way in Mississippi, Georgia, and a rest stop in South Carolina, but mostly it was just me and Corey and a ton of cigarettes.

We moved into a great little apartment where the patio looked out onto the pool. Corey was stationed on the USS Enterprise, so he spent ten days with me before he went out to sea for a month and a half. My job was to find a job. I worked at that tirelessly with the newspaper and any and all leads I had from networking back home and with people I met. I ate a lot of green beans and ramen noodles. And right before Corey returned home, I had a job. I had my college degree, a job, and my man. We even had a cat. We went to concerts and bars and parties and spent Sundays eating donuts and smoking cigarettes in bed. (Corey and I have always been a class act.)

We were married June 12th of 1999. It was a big wedding. Big. Lots of people came. We were married in a park back home in Arlington. Outside in June in Texas, and I wore hose. Not the best decision. Our wedding was beautiful in so many ways. It really was. But I felt a lot of pressure. I think every bride feels that way. I felt a lot of pressure to make everyone happy. And that pretty much was and is who I had been my whole life, so this role came easy to me. But that day in June it was so difficult. Once you have met the person who really sees you, the way Corey sees me, it becomes so much harder to hide behind your default role. I wanted to have both my dads walk me down the aisle. And I felt so much pressure that this was not ok. My dad and I had enjoyed a great relationship all through college, but here I was back at home, and I couldn't navigate the roads. I couldn't navigate how to handle my whole family being in the same place at once. Who do I please? I crushed my dad that day. I crushed him. I spoke volumes in that decision. The shame I felt was overwhelming. I quit talking to my dad shortly thereafter. How do you look someone in the eye, who has loved you your whole life whether they could see you or not, after you willfully chose to hurt them? You just don't. And a coldness started to move into my heart that was big and deep.

Corey finished up his six years in the Navy to move us back to Arlington so he could go to college. We spent the next four years with Corey working full time at hospitals or surgery centers as a scrub tech, a trade he received in the Navy. He went to college full time at night. I tried my hand at recruiting for a while, and over lunch with Mac one day he asked me what I was doing with my life. I told him I had no idea what type of job I wanted, and he said words that would change the course of my life: "You're a teacher." I gave two weeks notice and began teaching a Life Skills class to severe and profoundly handicapped students. I taught reading and communication, and my days were filled with the pure joy and absolute struggles that can only come from hanging out with mentally retarded kids. And I was thrown back into that place inside of me that had only existed when I taught Sunday school for Mission Arlington, loving on people and helping people who needed some extra love. Help could bring out the best in me. And Jesus was there in that classroom. Everyday. He was there every moment I taught, speaking so much love through the words of Norma Morales, my teaching assistant.

Jesus worked overtime those four years. Norma Morales loved me so completely. She would leave devotionals on my desk, and I would read them because I loved her. I listened to her. She made me play Christian music in my classroom. I asked her questions about God. She prayed for me. And she would tell me that Jesus had mighty plans for my life. I was so far from perfect. I was so far from being the woman so in love with a Savior that I would walk any road He asked me to walk. You could talk to Norma about anything—cheese, music, Puerto Rico, dominoes—and the next thing you knew she was telling you about Jesus. And it wasn't in a pushy way either. Jesus was her whole life. We worked with kiddos who had all sorts of disabilities, and oh, how she loved them. She loved the ones who could talk and hold funny conversations. She loved the ones that would never speak and were violent. She loved the students who were wheelchair bound and barely made eye contact. And the students responded to that love. I had never met anyone like this woman. And she just loved me. She was proud of me. I loved being with her. I loved listening to her. And I was drawn to her. I look back now and see that I was drawn to Jesus in her. She was the most gracious and giving and funny person I had ever met. And I loved seeing her every single day. And I got really near to Jesus during those four years, but I just couldn't do it. I just couldn't completely commit. And I could talk it sometimes. I could read and listen and think, but I couldn't give Jesus my life. I could dance around, and I totally wanted that peace that Norma had, but following Jesus couldn't be nearly as exciting as partying all the time.

Corey and I carried the party lifestyle straight into our marriage. We got married and quit sleeping around but nothing else really changed. We drank, and drank heavily, almost every night. We spent our money going out and headed home after the bars closed or headed out to another party or would have an impromptu party at our house. We met so many people and would make friends with anyone and everyone we were drinking near. However, this lead to some pretty hefty drunk arguments. But for the most part we were happy. My whole world could be crashing down, and Corey and I still could find a way to laugh and have a good time. He was working hard and I was working hard. We were still super young. It was ok to come home and throw up in the yard or get a ride home from a complete stranger or have screaming drunken arguments at 3 AM. And I never really thought much more of our life. We would party forever. That's who we were, and someday, hopefully, we would make it to Austin where we could raise some barefoot kiddos and live the dream.

In 2003, Corey was finishing up his last year of college. This was an enormous feat. He had given up on the idea of college after dropping out of high school twice. Also, we were pregnant with Jacob. We were beyond happy with our life, living in a little house with hard wood floors, baby on the way, Corey graduating, and me teaching. It was really great. If things had stayed just this way, we would have never been open to Jesus. If things had stayed this good, we could never have heard Him. Because things were good and in no need of changing, and we were happy and in no need of changing. And whenever we had annoyed my mom enough or made my mom worry enough, we would pop into church. Norma always made me listen to Christian music and I loved some of it. She gave me Christian books to read, so I could talk about some things. And I liked the whole concept of God with a plan. But Jesus as a Savior...well, that was too much, too far-fetched. Jesus as the only way—I still wasn't buying that one, and organized religion was something I could poke fun at on any given day. So I often stood on a fence, with loads of questions and tons of uneducated commentary. But life was good. So all those questions could wait, and I could still become angry at Jesus at the drop of a hat. And I could play any game I needed to play, because I had been playing games my whole life.

Jacob Corey Hooks was born November 25, 2003. And my heart exploded. I had never in my life felt so much tangible love. The moment I held him on my chest I was in love. The moment I heard him cry I would have given my life for him. I had never felt anything like this love, and I couldn't stop holding and loving and staring at this precious little baby who was loving me right back. It was unreal. It was unconditional. And it was instant.

And these immense emotions were sweeping over me. As I sat there and stared at my one-day-old baby, I could understand how my dad could say that he loved me. I could understand what he meant when he said that he loved me and had thought of me and how this emotion didn't subside with time or distance...how he knew exactly what I looked like and knew exactly who I was. He was my dad and time had passed from 5 years old to 13 years old, and he had missed a lot, but he did love me. And this revelation would change so much for me. I would desperately need to connect with my dad again. I could build this bridge. I could walk this road because now, one day into parenthood, my heart understood so much more than I ever had before about loving your kids. And Jesus was right there, allowing places and pieces in my heart to heal. Taking down the target I had been wearing since I was 5 years old saying that my dad never loved me. And a place inside my soul began to whisper to a little, long lost girl, "Wake Up."

I would reconnect with my dad and Dycee and Maureen when Jake was 3 months old. This was huge for me on so many levels. Now that I was a mommy, I was committed to this relationship, my family, in a whole new light. I was not a burden to my Nashville clan. They were just separated from me by time and distance, and the only one who could change that was me. There was so much love there. So much love waiting on my kids. So many apologies I needed to say. And I could not, and did not, worry about my mom. As my mom had grown in her faith over the years, she had gotten to a place with less fear and less insecurity. I think she had her eyes open and knew, in a different way, that I needed my family, all of my family, and this didn't take away her place in my life. It was a time of reconciliation and hope. It was a time to put away my anger and pick up the sadness I carried inside and say that I was sorry. It was good; and Nashville, and all the people I loved there and who absolutely loved me began to have the voice in my life they were meant to have. It was so good. Every girl needs her dad to love her...every girl. It is way more than a want. It is a need. And when we don't have it, or when we don't believe we have it, we are broken and shattered in a way that cuts so deep. But if we get a second chance for it to be revealed and felt and treasured, the little special dazzling princess in each of us wakes up from her deep sleep and sees the world a little better.

If I could have seen all that Jesus was orchestrating from Heaven during this time, I would have been floored. I would have seen everything the next two years would bring and would not try so hard to steer the ship. Jesus began to let our world fall apart. As parts of our life would come crashing down, very strategic parts of our life would become stronger and the places that we would desperately hold on to. Corey would graduate from college when Jake was 10 days old. I would finish out the school year teaching while Jake went to the world's greatest daycare at my parents' church. And the career hunt would begin with our sights set on money, money, money. He would begin a job in medical sales that held so much financial promise, and I would begin the crazy journey as a stay-at-home mom. And I would find out I was pregnant again when Jake was six months old.

This unexpected, back-to-back baby would rock our world a bit. Corey's job required him to be gone at all times of the day and night on a moment's notice, and our world began to rock a little more. I was sick almost the entire nine months of my pregnancy and our life was definitely not getting any easier. I did not have the peaceful voice of Norma Morales in my ear every day, which made matters even more stressful. We both spent money like it was water and began to accrue some pretty serious debt. We still went out together all the time, and our nights were dotted with pretty intense fights. Soon our mornings and afternoons were housing those same intense fights too. Before long, our marriage and our friendship and our love for each other was fading and fading fast.

And it was so painful, but I was keeping up my front. We never argued in public, and I never talked bad about my husband. I spent a lot of time with my friend, Malissa, who had a little boy just a month older than Jake. I would drive to her house, even though it was an hour away, and see her and her son and her mom, Robbin. And there was my peace. They talked about Jesus, and I could talk it with them because I knew enough. And I could get Jake dedicated in front of my parents' whole church. And I could tell people I was praying for them or praying with them or needing Jesus, but I couldn't surrender. And I could stand and stay with my friends who didn't believe and say that it all was brainwashing and Christians were imprisoned by their rules and regulations. Except for the select few, they were all a little crazy to me. And doesn't God just want us all to be happy anyway? I would play this game of fence hopping, and inside, my world was falling apart and I had no one to tell and no one to cry out to, but being halfway honest had always been comfortable. So as long as I knew what I believed, well, then we were all ok. But this motherhood thing was breaking me; and it was breaking me daily.

You see, when you have spent the majority of your life surviving life and saying whatever you need to say to get by and doing pretty much whatever you want and then this crazy love appears—If there is a heart beating in your chest, your priorities move. You don't have to survive, but this little life sure does. You don't have to have everything you want, but this little life sure does. You don't have to be happy, but man, it sure is great when this little life is happy. And this would be the dividing line Corey and I stood on, on many days. While he worked and took clients out and went to trainings around the country and went to dinners and didn't answer my calls much, I was sick at home with a little guy who called my cell phone "DaDa" and another little guy on the way. We truly just became a burden. Corey worked constantly and played just as much. I was still trying to be the "cool" wife—understanding about strip clubs, understanding about finances, which seemed more important to spend on clients than on groceries—and then I would explode out of nowhere. There was zero communication between us, but I had no one to talk to except Corey.

And just as Jesus would have it, I received in the mail one day an invitation to join a Kindermusik class for babies. This would be a rhythm and music class. It sounded funky and vaguely hippyish (something I could stand behind). And I was only getting more and more pregnant with a little one at home who was into everything, so a place where we could meet moms in our area who were into music for babies sounded really good. We joined the class, and my world got a jolt when I walked through the doors of the teacher's house. It took just under five minutes for me to realize I was in a Kindermusik class with all Christians who went to my mom and Mac's church. They all knew my mom from choir or Mac from being a deacon. My entire fight or flight response was going off like crazy, and I needed to quit the class as soon as possible. But we kept laughing the entire hour, and at the very end the gals invited me to lunch at Luby's. Unfortunately, I enjoyed myself more than I imagined possible and went back week after week for the nicest girls, Luby's, and a friendship that would change my life.

Kathryn was my least likely friend—a friendship only Jesus could orchestrate. She was the piano player at my mom's church and had lived a life of making wonderful choices while she followed Jesus. We had nothing in common. But it was undeniable how much we got along. She started inviting me over to her house, and we would let our boys play while we talked and talked and laughed and sometimes I cried. I would tell her the truth about my marriage. I would tell her that things were not going well. I would tell her about the lies about finances and the late nights and the parties and the fights. I would tell her the truth while it was happening, and I didn't wait for it to get pretty or better. And I was also honest with her about my beliefs. I told her that I didn't believe Jesus was the Son of God, I didn't believe in Hell, I didn't believe in organized religion, and I didn't believe the Bible. And yet, I knew she believed. I just didn't play any games with her, and here was the kicker: she did not judge me. She didn't agree with me, but she never once put me down or quit inviting me over or treated me like an idiot. She just befriended a sinner. She just loved a hurting girl. She just extended her arms as wide as she could, and unbeknownst to me, offered the arms of a Carpenter King to fall into whenever I was falling apart. She was the hands and feet of Jesus. You see, years before, Mac asked Kathryn to pray for his daughter, Jackie. And when I entered that Kindermusik class, Kathryn knew beyond a shadow of a doubt that Jesus was setting up an important meeting and treated it as such. She treated the there-is-a-million-ways-to-heaven-cigarette-smoking-yep-I've-slept-with-everyone-Jesus-was-just-a-nice-guy-I-hate-goody-two-shoes-Christians-just-like-you girl as a divine appointment, and I couldn't get enough. Kathryn was my safe haven inside my storm that no one knew I was enduring.

By the time Jude Cameron Hooks arrived on March 16th, 2005, my marriage was in the gutter. Cory and I were barely hanging on to what was left of a marriage that only had loads of alcohol and too many screaming arguments to count anymore. We hung up on each other, cussed each other out, slammed doors, yelled in the driveway, ignored each other, and just plain hated each other behind closed doors. But since Corey and I were cut from the same cloth, we both knew how to fake it when anyone else was around. The only thing that really kept us together was this happy little baby named, Jude, who had so many random medical issues and false alarms. We were a united front when it came to Jude.

Jude had his first surgery at 10 days old when his circumcision went wrong and a surgeon had to remove the plastibell (don't know if those are even allowed anymore). Corey and I were there together, holding hands as our itty-bitty baby was carried into surgery. Before too long, doctors believed his soft spot had closed too early, and we went to a neurosurgeon together to get a sonogram of his precious head. Jude had horrible stomach issues and could not gain weight. And we would be together worrying about this one little boy. We have often said that if Jude hadn't had a myriad of health issues and scares we would not have stayed together. But Jesus knew what He was doing. He was holding us together in one little area and allowing all the other stresses to tear our marriage down to the core. And when we got to the core there wasn't much left because the love was gone, and there was no real foundation to begin with.

You know, Jesus is funny. His huge sense of humor is revealed as He draws you close to Him. Make no mistake; there are things He does to let you know later on down the road that He was holding the cards. My two oldest sons are named Jacob and Jude. The entire time we were crumbling and searching and hurting, people would often comment on our sons' Biblical names. We had no idea. I had no idea there was a Jude in the Bible. I knew about Jacob in the Bible only after Norma had explained it, but when we named Jude we just played "Hey Jude" a lot and named him after Judah (which is a girl name to me since Judah is a girl...yes, I know it is a man in the Bible). Jude was fitting. Anyone with the name Jude would certainly be cool. And with these two biblical names, people often asked us what church we went to or commented on how fitting that we had done Old and New Testament names. Jesus kept His name walking in and out of our lives by intentionally naming our sons. I am sure He smiled and smiled every time the conversations would start and we would squirm.

As things got worse and worse in our marriage, I began to make a plan. It was summer. I was home with two little boys. Jake was my easy-going, barrel-chested little guy with blonde hair and blue eyes and the chubbiest cheeks in the known universe. Jude was my skinny, scrawny itty-bitty who woke up smiling at the crack of dawn, never napped, and never stopped. The two of them held my heart in their hands. As Corey was working hard to make his career in sales take off, he would sometimes choose clients over groceries. My mom bought us diapers and peanut butter and jelly more times than I can count. I would travel with my little family to Nashville that summer and Corey and I would fight the entire trip. We took family pictures that trip. There we are with the two most adorable children, smiling, sitting close together and no one knew how far we were drifting apart. But Jesus is good y'all, and as I was planning to leave Corey after Christmas, He was kicking it into high gear.

I enrolled my Jake at Fielder Road Baptist Church for pre-school. He was just under two years old, but I needed some time with just the baby, and it seemed like a good choice. So many people I knew sent their kids to that pre school. Jake would bring home artwork with scripture, and I would read it. Jake would bring home little devotionals, and I would read them. The moms in the hall were so kind and they talked about Jesus. The teachers prayed for my son and knew my name and all about Jude. We had been there less than a month, and I looked forward to my time in the hallway with all these women on Tuesdays and Thursdays more than anything. Kathryn and I had joined The Little Gym together, and we still spent our time together laughing. She was still the one person I let my guard down around, and I had shared with her how much I was hurting in my marriage. Malissa and her mom, Robbin, were still a constant place of peace and inspiration and love. I look back and see that I should have just been honest with them too, but I wanted so badly to turn my boat around or just let it capsize. Honesty was a luxury I had never been able to afford. And then there was my mom. She had started picking up my boys on Sunday mornings to take them to church. She said that I could use a break, and I didn't have to attend since I had made it clear, to her especially, how much I was not buying this Christianity crap. So, I would get my boys ready and send them on with her. Every Sunday. I had told her many times that I didn't want her taking them anymore, but a tired mom can't refuse free babysitting, so I would send them with her whether I believed in Jesus or not because sleep was like gold with two babies at home.

Jesus was working all these things out. He was planting 90 million seeds a day when I look back on it. He was using every single moment to make us see Him. He was keeping us together just enough while we were drifting apart because He had this mighty plan. He was about to make it all work out, but I had no clue. I felt like I was going under. I felt like I could not take much more of a marriage that lost all it's love and romance two years before. I felt like I could not take all my fake and phony and half truths, and I was clinging to Kathryn and I was clinging to the hallways at Fielder Road and I was clinging to the peace found with my friend Malissa and I was clinging to the things Norma had said were true, and maybe, just maybe God had a mighty plan, but where was it? I would say daily my positive thinking mantra about how I was bringing all good things into my life. I would listen again and again to the psychics I had taped. I was reading my horoscope. I was desperate. And little did I know that Corey was desperate too. And as more and more fights began to rage in our home and the line between us and hate became thinner and thinner, Jesus was getting ready for the appearance of a lifetime.

On September 8, 2005, everything came to a dramatic climax. I had put the boys to bed, and poured myself a drink. Corey was inside working on a cover letter for a new sales position he was applying for at a different company. I was rocking in my purple rocking chair, smoking a cigarette, being alone, being quiet. Corey came outside and we started to argue. We had gotten to that really really horrible point in a marriage where within two words we could be in an argument. I got up and went inside. I walked back to our bedroom, and Corey had his cover letter still opened on the computer. As I read his words, my blood started to boil. He had actually written that he wanted this job because he wanted to get closer to God and to his family. What? I knew this man, and the last thing he cared about was me or God, and I was not going to let him get away with lying. I stormed outside and began an epic, loud monologue about him and who he was and who he was not and how dare he write such a lie in a cover letter using me and the kids and God to get a job.

And Corey started to cry.

My husband is not a crier. I have seen him cry less than ten times over the course of our entire marriage. He might get a little choked up, but tears rarely fall. So, I should have been floored. I should have cared. But I was beyond caring. I was beyond hoping my marriage would turn around. We were just two people now. Just two people with two little boys and so much water under so many bridges. And yet here we were on our front porch having an enormous argument as usual, and I knew Corey was about to tell me something huge. I knew he was about to confess something huge. I knew with every fiber in my being that this night, September 8th was going to mark our end. And I was ready. I braced myself for his next sentence that I was sure was going to tear the last few nails out of the last few boards of the last few standing walls of what was left of our marriage.

"Jackie, I don't know what's happening to me, but I think I am supposed to go inside and ask Jesus to be my Savior."

This moment is branded in time. This moment stands still in my memory. This moment was so calm and peaceful and shocking with the rug that I was desperately trying to still stand on being finally ripped from beneath my feet. As I put out my cigarette, I looked at my husband sitting in his chair. I looked at the man who had spent his entire young life in church not caring or believing a word that was said. He didn't hate Jesus or God or Christians. He just didn't believe them, and he didn't care either. And all the words that Jesus had painstakingly tucked into his heart all the years that he had sat in pews or uncomfortable Sunday School chairs came rushing out on this front porch. He could have said anything. He could have said he was having an affair and the words would have gone down easier. But instead he said that Jesus was supposed to be his Savior, and I was left speechless on the front porch with my husband who I didn't love and Jesus who sure seemed to love us enough to just show up on a random Thursday when we needed Him most.

I was done. I was finished. I was over searching. I stood on that front porch silent. I felt every piece of that moment. It was just cool enough. It was just quiet enough. And here we were with Jesus who was speaking straight to my heart saying, I can do anything. I can come get you in the middle of your mess. I knew my positive mantra had never showed up on my front porch. My Buddha had never shown up. My tarot cards had never ripped apart our messy lives and stood with us in our imperfections. My psychic tapes had never come to save us. And here was my husband of all people surrendering his life to Jesus. I was tired. I was broken. I had no fight left in me. If I had a tad less pride I would have fallen to my knees, but instead I held on to the porch railing and felt my Jesus walk into my life through the saving grace Corey was grabbing hold of on our front porch in Arlington, TX.

"I don't think I'm qualified to help you with this," were the only words that came out of my mouth.

The events of this night still seem unbelievable to me when I look back on them. I still can feel the shock that swept over my body. It was such a physical feeling of absolute disbelief when I heard my husband tell me he felt like Jesus was supposed to be his Savior. This disbelief was followed by enormous peace—waves of peace and this crazy knowledge that we were going to follow Jesus. There are moments in your life where you know your whole life has just changed. Some of those life-changing moments are really good like having a baby or getting married or starting your dream job or quitting a horrible job; some of those life-changing moments are really hard like losing someone you love to illness or finding out your spouse is having an affair or finally being honest with everyone you know. This moment was the most powerful moment I have ever felt in my life. And I instantly felt so worn out. I felt like I had been fighting a fight for so long by myself, and I was just plain finished with the fighting. I wonder what this scene looked like from heaven. How many angels were gathered on that front porch too? How many prayers were answered in that one moment? How many amens were breathed out through decades of prayers? Jesus had heard them all, and He had come to change everything.

As we walked inside I told Corey we needed to call my mom and Mac because I didn't know what to do next. So, the first time I prayed with my husband was on my knees on the hardwood floor in our living room with my mom and Mac on the other end of the line. I don't remember what they said. I don't remember what we said. All I know is that there were lots of tears, and I was holding Corey's hand.

In case anyone ever wonders, I married the perfect man for me. He is the strongest willed human I have ever come across. He is married to the strongest willed woman. And together we are raising some of the strongest willed children this side of the Universe. But in all that strong will, he is wise. It is not this daily wisdom that makes me feel like I am married to a TV character. It is a wisdom that comes spilling all over our lives when we need it most. That night after praying and crying, I was dumbfounded with, "So, what now?" Corey said that we had to find a Bible, and the search began. It took awhile, but we found one in a box in the garage. Corey had been given a book called, "Forty Days of Worship" as one of my mom and Mac's attempts to get us back on the right path. It was written by Dennis Wiles, who would later become our pastor. We did this Bible study together for the next forty days. Corey made sure we put our feet on the path before us, and he made sure we started walking before we could turn around or sit down or give up.

And that weekend we went to church. We did not church shop. We just went to my mom and Mac's church because that was the only church we knew and the church we had gone to when we were younger. We swore we would never make it our church home because we wanted to start fresh. But Jesus was in that church, and we never left. Each Sunday my least likely friend, Kathryn, who went to the same church as my mom and Mac would meet us or her husband would meet us and show us to different Sunday School classes in our age group. We enjoyed all of them. But when it came time to make a decision, Corey stood firm about where we should go. He chose a "Nearly/Newly" married class. I could have shot him. Here we were, married for six years with two kids and he wanted us to be with newlyweds or engaged couples with no kids. But Corey said that we had no idea how to live out a biblical marriage, and we had to start somewhere. And there we were, the old smoking sinners in a class with some of the nicest people. It felt awkward at first. It felt overwhelming too. But Corey was right, and we were supposed to get some basics in our life to rebuild before we ever could start over.

Jesus can do anything, y'all. Jesus is big enough to do anything. He can step in and save two broken and beat people and save a marriage all at the same time. He can show up anywhere and at anytime He wants to show up. And I have a feeling He does it all the time. He walks into our mess and just loves us. That love is so powerful and so needed that it changes everything if you let it. And the journey I was embarking upon with my husband, hands down, is the best road I have ever and will ever walk—the road we just keep walking with Jesus. But it all had to start somewhere, and for us, it started in a failing marriage with no hope left at all. It started in my darkest moments when I was so comfortable with charades that I could barely remember what was truth or fiction anymore. It started when I didn't know I was looking for Him and I found out He was searching for me. Jesus found me on my front porch with my pride, my defiance, my lost hope, my broken dreams, my worn out sad mess of a life, and He loved me. He stepped into my life through the absolute miracle of my husband's salvation. And I will never be the same.

CHAPTER FOUR

Grace

Grace catches you off guard. Grace doesn't make sense and it is typically so unexpected that we almost deny grace the effects it can have in our life because grace is just so grace filled. A few months into our extreme marriage makeover God started asking me to have another baby. We had our two beautiful sons already, and we were still in the stage of rebuilding where you realize you have zero viable tools in your tool belt. We had all the tools we needed to bail out, scream at one another, blame and justify our wrongs, but we were missing the tools to love the way Jesus wanted us to love. The rebuilding part itself felt overwhelming and humiliating all at the same time. And here comes Jesus into all of my prayers to be able to possibly love my husband again with His crazy idea of another baby. I loved the idea of having another child, but having that new baby with my husband seemed like a deal breaker. To make matters even worse, Corey wasn't on board at all. He was happily raising two boys and working hard to make sure we COULD build a new marriage that would stand the test of time and more trials that were sure to come. The "project" we were dealing with was an enormous undertaking, but Jesus wouldn't let the new baby thing go...and He began pounding down the doors of my heart relentlessly.

Everywhere I went it was like; "Have Another Baby" was posted on every wall. We could be listening to a sermon on tithing, and somehow I left with tears running down my face talking about having another baby. I could be in the grocery line and suddenly somehow someone would strike up a conversation with me about having another baby, and end up telling me I should go for it. The songs on the radio, soccer games, any magazine article, a box of popcorn, taking a walk, calling to change our cable order...you name it, it all screamed "HAVE ANOTHER BABY!" I was convinced. And Corey was not even on the fence. So, I did what I had just learned might move mountains, and I asked him to just pray about it. So, he did. He prayed from December till one night in March. He walked in from a Bible Study, sat down and said the words which are music to every gal's ears, "Honey, I was wrong, and you were right. We are supposed to have another baby." Three weeks later we were pregnant.

I began to plan for my third boy. I needed to have a boy. I knew boys. I was good at the rough and tumble of boys. I had boy things. This would be so much easier if I just had a boy. And every once in a while I would linger in my thoughts about having a little girl...pink, tutus, bows, nail polish, dance, sparkles...and I would shut it out and think about the third boy. We easily had our boy name picked out. It had sat on a shelf in all the other baby naming. The girl name was not coming so easily. We had lists on the computer, asked friends...nothing seemed to fit. So, I planned more for a boy and actually asked people to pray we had a boy...and every so often I would look at a little dress and my heart would ache in a way I had never felt before...a sadness that hurt so deep in the middle of Target...and I would hurry over to the blue section and feel at home.

It happened the week before we found out if we were having a boy or a girl (yes, we are the couple that has to know...no surprises here...I'm a planner by nature...it can be annoying at times). I was sitting in my Thursday night Bible Study and my grandmother, Eleanor Grace had just recently passed away. People always referred to her as "Gracie" or "Eleanor Grace", and my friend was telling a sweet story about the last time she saw my grandmother and she called her, "Grace". It was like a lightning bolt to my heart. Immediately I texted my husband and said, "Her name is Grace. Grace Evelyn Hooks." He loved it too. I imagined for one second a little peaceful, poised, girl with a bun in her hair and little smart clothes, sitting quietly. If it was Grace she would be graceful and gentle and calming and fluffy and frilly and she might eat dainty food with her pinky in the air. Grace was quiet and comforting. It was perfect. But I was still having a boy. So, I pushed the thought out of my head and imagined my stinky feet house of boys, loud and obnoxious with their pony tailed, no makeup wearing mom being the perfect fit.

Grace Evelyn Hooks was born January 5th, 2007.

Grace left the hospital in a sea of pink. She wore a bow a few hours after she was born. There was a new pink car seat, new crib, fancy pink bedding, a pink room, cascades of ruffles and rhinestones crept into our life almost instantly. I am not dumb. I get it and I know what people expect. I talked about how great it was to finally have my precious girl, and I meant it. I really did. I talked about how excited I was to do Strawberry Shortcake, My Little Ponies, paint toenails and pierce ears. And I meant it. I was over the moon having this adorable, bundle of cuteness join our family. We moved into our new, big house a month after Grace was born and a friend of my step dad redecorated Grace's room as a present for the first girl. The room was gorgeous and yummy and so girly. Grace was a wanted addition. Grace was beautiful. Grace was special. But as Grace continued to grow and get more personality, it became obvious that Grace was nothing like the calm little girl I had seen in my head. If Grace loved you, she loved you enormously. She would hug so tight. She would hold hands so often. Grace was loud. Grace was quirky. Grace was ferocious and determined. At 9 months old dressed as a kitty cat princess (her brothers picked the costume) she WALKED up to the doors with the other trick or treaters and held out her bucket. Grace knew what she wanted and she was confident enough to get it. Grace was not what I had expected.

We have a picture of Grace during her first dance recital. She was not even two years old (don't judge), and it was the finale where the entire dance studio did one big dance together. It was called the "Daddy Daughter Dance", and the daddies would sign up to learn an awesome dance routine with their daughters, full costume, full choreography and it was the highlight of the whole recital. You are laughing and crying as you watch these dads working so hard and their daughters for one song montage being little girls in awe of their hero….ok…or mortified. But it is precious. Corey had gone to Friday night rehearsals, he had his amazing 70's era costume and he was dancing like crazy with Grace. And in the middle of the whole chaotic, perfectly timed number, Grace broke free and ran out on to a little platform center stage and started dancing like nobody's business. She danced her heart out. Grace took center stage, and the entire performance changed. All eyes on this tiny, unexpected, pigtailed girl in red tights who had stolen the spotlight. And as tears streamed down my face, I heard a familiar voice in my head, "This is who I created you to be." And as everyone was hugging and laughing and talking about my girl, I was putting the finishing touches on the 82 foot layer of ice around my heart so that I could survive having Grace in my life. It was too much. Grace was just too much.

By the time Grace was 2 ½ years old, I was unraveling pretty solidly. I had a saying with my kiddos, "If I can't see you, I can't save you." Yes, this is disturbing. I would be anywhere and begin to have a panic feeling wash over me...parking lots, grocery stores, restaurants, church...and if my kiddos were out of my line of vision, I would have to quickly account for all of them. I would tell them, in a shaky voice, "If I can't see you, I can't save you." I'm sure to the other moms I may have appeared a touch neurotic, or maybe they never noticed. But these head counts were starting to take place in greater and greater numbers as Grace grew. I began to push really hard for Grace to be a "Daddy's Girl" too. I needed to distance myself from her. Because I knew what no one else knew: Someone was going to steal her. Someone was going to take her from me, and she wouldn't know to run, and I wouldn't be able to save her and I could not recover from this...

I began counting a lot. I began counting the seconds if the kids were in the backyard, and I was going to grab popsicles from the kitchen. I gave myself 30 seconds. 1...2...3...4...5...and I was running, grabbing popsicles, wresting them out of their wrappers, hurrying to the backyard because all it would take was a second and she would be gone. I began taking note of everyone. By 2009, a play date at the park was like a scene in "The Bourne Identity" for me. I was memorizing faces of the people at the park, what they wore, where they were seated and what routes I would have to take to rescue my daughter from them. I had efficient master plans worked out at any given moment. The headcounts were merciless for me. If I can't see you, I can't save you. And save you I must, because no one but me saved myself. It was overwhelming. I felt like I couldn't breathe at times. But I knew what no one else knew: The worst thing you can imagine just might happen. I had to cut off all feelings I had for this precious gift of Grace so that I could focus on keeping her safe. Oh, and I had to fake normal and happy. I pretty much walked on a little tightrope inside a mighty hurricane every day. And no one knew. And I couldn't tell. And life went on as usual.

The summer of 2009 a few monumental things happened. First, I celebrated 10 years married to Corey Hooks...wow. We were in a whole new marriage. Redeemed. Transformed. This man who loved his family and loved me and didn't care about climbing a crazy corporate ladder or wearing only name brands was someone new. He was calmer. He was funnier. He was truly the head of our household, and I trusted him with decisions like I never had before. He was diligently digging us out of a financial ditch, being an amazing father and this unbelievable rock of a husband. We had walked some tough roads, and that summer we truly celebrated a decade together. We renewed our vows in a small ceremony with the people who had walked with us on this road to being a "New Creation". It was outside, with colorful handmade paper fans, flip flops, a three tiered yellow wedding cake, punch and paper lanterns and my kids hanging from our legs and hips the whole time. Jesus, over the last couple of years had created a safe place in my marriage. I remember telling Corey, I have never felt so safe before in my life. Second, I was in a Bible Study. This was nothing new. I had been in a weekly women's Bible Study for a few years now. We were asked on the first night of this new study, to pair up with someone and pray together. I ended up with a girl I barely new, and for some reason, and I still don't know why, I just asked for that super down deep prayer...not the Sunday School I can share this with anyone prayer, but the prayer that you try not to even tell yourself and you are hoping that Jesus doesn't really know everything because if He knew this about you, He would surely call it quits. And I asked her to pray for me because I could not love my daughter. I told her I felt like there was an 82 foot thick cover of ice on my heart, and I knew below it was a river alive and filled with love. I just couldn't get to it. I told her I had been abducted when I was 6 years old by a stranger and I knew this same thing was going to happen to Grace. And I had to protect her. And I needed prayer. I was falling apart. And she prayed for me. Really, really prayed for me. And she honored my secret. And she didn't stop praying once the Bible Study ended. God gave me a person to tell, and she did not treat me like I was crazy, but her prayers...and just the knowledge that her prayers were out there...held me so tightly. I cannot describe how desperately the terrified pieces of me needed one person to know. And finally, at the end of the summer of 2009, I had to go back to work. It was definitely not my plan to go back to work before all my kids were in school, but Corey told me we couldn't continue without me working and I cried and cried and cried some more, but I told him yes because I trusted him. Then I prayed for peace and that God would let me wake up in the morning and know that I was on the right path. And I woke up peaceful, and a job opened up at Arlington High School, where my mom taught, where I had graduated years before, that very same day, and it was right around the corner from where my kiddos would go to elementary school. And we had a friend who could watch Jude and Grace three days a week, and another friend available to take Jude and Grace home from preschool two days a week. And I would not be able to see my kids all day long, and I would have to rely on God to save them which was really hard for me, but it was the road I had just been placed on. And everything fell into place, and everything was ok. And God set me down in this really safe space. He gave me a husband that was totally and obviously a new man, one person to pray for me and an act of obedience that would change so many things about my life and my path. God filled my life with peace, and allowed the strongest winds of my hurricane to start to chip away at the ice I had lived with all my life. And it all was going to be ok.

When I started work that fall semester I was actually excited. I ran into people I had not seen in years, and teachers who had taught me in high school were now my colleagues. I loved the team in the special education department I was on, and felt an instant connection to so many of the women I worked with...days were full of laughter and tears. When you have a good team you might drive each other a little crazy and love each other all the same. It was back to work and I was in a good place. I taught Sunday school alongside my husband, we had a Bible Study meeting in our home, we had cleaned up so much of our life and we were on track to clean up our frivolous finances too. But the storm kept raging inside of me, and the ice around my heart I had lived with comfortably for most of my life began to not be so comfortable. And the ice was cracking, and there was nothing I could do about it. Life was rolling along and better than ever, and I was still falling apart secretly. Insomnia became my constant companion that fall. I would wake up two to three times a night and have to go check my children's rooms. I was convinced someone was going to break in and take them in the middle of the night. They would be gone forever while I slept. So, no sleep. Just awake, by myself, making sure that I could save them. And if you have been hiding inside yourself for decades like me, you do what you do best, and hide further inside your "life skit". I became more vulnerable and honest about the poor choices I had made in my life, I tried to help as many people as I could, praying for others, going to church any time the doors were open, trying to consider every trial pure joy and memorize scripture and join PTA...anything to avoid myself. Stay busy. Stay focused on others. Stay strong. Stay calm. Stay distant. Ask others how they are doing. Turn the attention away from me. Make people laugh. Make people happy. Make people forget they didn't know anything about what was going on with you...and it just wasn't working anymore.

I was crowded in Grace's junior bed one night, tucking her in. I was not dumb. I know how to go through the motions seamlessly. I was trying to pretend I was comfortable with the snuggling and silly conversation, and I was trying to remember to play with her hair. Grace looked at me, eye to eye with her big brown eyes and said in her tiny little voice, "Mommy, you are the icing and I am the sprinkles." I kissed her abruptly on the nose and got out of there as fast as I could. I walked into the living room, where my husband was seated on the couch. I felt like I had been punched in the soul. I told him what Grace had just said to me...the icing and sprinkles cuteness of it all. And Corey asked if I had just eaten her up...and I said no. He asked if I was ok...and I said no. And from there I would open my mouth and 29 years of silence came to an end. 29 years of closing my eyes and moving on. 29 years of headcounts and making survival plans in every crowded venue. 29 years of surviving at a distance from every person I had ever loved. 29 years of being just fine. Just ok. Just living. 29 years of laughter and silliness on the outside, and an ice river that was now at flood stage on the inside. 29 years had passed since the day in the woods, and I was still living inside the wreckage...by myself...thinking that I had survived. Clearly I had only survived and missed out on some valuable living.

And the tears wouldn't stop. And I don't even know exactly all I said, but when I was finished, and Corey knew everything, he said the best words ever, "You make so much more sense now." You know, grace is just so unexpected. And then he held me, and told me how sorry he was for everything that had happened to me. He didn't interrogate me, or back away from the big old mess standing in front of him. He just loved me. And I was still breathing. And he knew everything. And God had given me a man who created for me a safe place where I could consider getting better. He gave me a man who was willing to walk with me, see all my broken places and offer to carry me if my feet failed. That's the kind of man God creates. And he did not push me over the next couple of months, but he didn't let me forget that I needed to figure out what Jesus wanted me to do. And I began to wake him up with me in the middle of the night, and tell him I needed to go check on the kids. He would say that they were fine, and this house was safe with an alarm, but if I needed to go check, so I could go back to sleep then I should go check. And I would go check the house, but for the first time in my life someone knew I was up checking the house, making sure my kids were not stolen. Someone knew my crazy secrets, and they saw that it was because I was broken. And for the first time in my life it was ok to be broken because anyone who is human would fall apart if they were abducted by a stranger when they were six years old and terrorized in the woods. And I felt for the first time in my life like I was normal for being broken.

So, I was making it through the fall of 2009. Part of me literally thought that if I shared my gunk with a couple of people that the ice would melt and I would be finished. As easy as pie. I spoke the secret password, the ice melted, Indiana Jones found the treasure at the bottom of the ice river, maybe Harry Potter showed up and did some magic, and poof, healed life. Move on and new story. But it wasn't working that way. I just had a safe place to go when I started feeling like I needed to build an army bunker and stash my kiddos in it, but my husband wasn't Jesus...and only Jesus was going to fix this. I was being the strong willed child of my Savior for the time being, and had decided to not pray about the matter at all or seek His will about the matter either because hey, ignorance is the best defense ever written. In spite of all this, in December, I decided to take a quick girl's trip to visit my best and oldest friend down in Austin, TX. Judah has been my best friend since I was five. I don't have to explain anything to her. I don't have to act normal...she was there before my life fell apart and she has been there since. So, Grace and I packed up, headed to Austin to visit Aunt Judah. We really just did what Judah and I do best: good coffee, good conversation and good music...play us some Indigo Girls and we are singing at the top of our lungs knowing every single word. We had tucked Grace in for the night and sat out on her back porch with a pack of cigarettes and a bottle of wine. We were having our normal endless conversation (Judah and I both talk a lot...and I mean a whole lot), when Judah said something that poured such truth out on the table of my life.

"Jackie, you make me sad. You could tell your whole life story, and you wouldn't even cry. And your life story is sad."

And I was caught off guard by the truth. And I was choking on uncontrollable tears. And I was called out by the one person who was allowed to call me out, and the girl who hadn't smoked in almost three years picked up a pack of cigarettes and let the last chip fall on the table. "Judah, I can't love my daughter. And I know, if I keep things going just like this, she will grow up to be cold and distant and a little too harsh...she will be just like me. And she won't know why. And she won't have any reason to have all these "issues"...but it will be my legacy. And she will say she was never that close to her mom, and if she has a daughter someday she will push her away too..." Judah didn't sugar coat. Judah didn't say that I was a good mom. Judah simply said that I was right, and I needed to figure out what to do to get help. She agreed that this path, although it was so much better than the way I grew up, was not good enough, was not healthy enough for my girl. We both knew that I could point to 982 ways that Corey and I had raised the bar of parenting in our own family, but raising the bar wasn't going to lead to children who were whole. Raising the bar just meant that they would be better, but Jesus didn't die on the cross for our lives to be better. Jesus died on the cross for our lives to be radically transformed into His image. And His image would never say, "I cannot love my daughter because of the fear I have that something might happen to her. So, I just don't love her." Jesus will completely forgive us for our short comings, but He is never ok with us giving up. He is never ok with us giving in. He is, however, completely ok with us giving everything over to Him, and saying, "I trust you Jesus to fix it all. And I will do whatever it takes to put my feet right behind yours."

I drove the 4 ½ hours back from Austin the next morning with complete resolution to ask Jesus what He wanted me to do to find victory in this mess. He had walked me this far. He had been so gracious. He had been careful with me. He had allowed me to see, just for a second, if I would trust Him, He would heal me. And I was finally willing to say, I was in desperate need of some healing. The outside was pretty cleaned up (except for those few cigarettes in Austin, but hey, it was nervous breakdown worthy), and Grace was quietly asleep in the backseat. I could look in the rearview mirror the whole drive home and see her sleeping, mouth wide open, blonde spiral curls everywhere, totally at peace...totally unaware that the lady in the front seat had risked every piece of her soul to save her from a 29 year old walk to the woods. The lady in the front seat had battled endless memories, demons and darkness all to save my Grace, my precious mess of the loudest beauty...my little girl... from MY life. And the lady in that front seat was finished. I was tired. I was tired of working so hard to simply not live my life to the fullest. I was tired of missing out on all the good things Jesus had planned for my future, just so I could make sure Grace Evelyn Hooks never lived my past. I was tired of loving my daughter from the other side of a ten foot pole. I was tired. I drove that road home in pure joy, knowing that Jesus would heal me and my family. I didn't know how, but I knew He would.

Kay was one of my Sunday school teachers. She led women's Bible Studies in her home too, and I had been sitting on her living room floor with Anna when we had been asked to pray with another girl the summer before. She is one of those women who walks abruptly into the kitchen of your house, makes herself at home, rocks your babies if they need it, scolds your children, hands you scripture every twenty two seconds, gives you a list of prayers she has prayed for you with smiley faces next to the ones she watched Jesus faithfully answer, offers some unsolicited advice, hands you a mountain of must read books and leaves you stunned and changed all in the same minute. You may have met a woman like her...if you have, you know, she will do almost anything to help another woman on her Jesus Journey. I had begun to pray that Jesus would reveal to me what His plan was to move me toward being freedom from my past. Every time I would pray, I would see Kay's face and feel like I was supposed to do a one on one Bible Study with her. Well, that was totally inconvenient. I didn't like the thought of that at all. I liked big groups where I could offer advice and share a story or two from my own life, but never really get to what was crushing me. Never really share my secrets. And if it was just Kay and I then I was basically out of luck because I knew this woman, and she would not let you tip toe into the shallow end...she would push you off the diving board and teach you how to swim. But Jesus would not let it alone. I finally told Kay I was praying about doing, "Breaking Free" with her and I was asking Jesus who all to invite. And I would pray and plead at the feet of Jesus to please throw some other girls in the mix, and He would always reassure me that it was going to be just Kay and me and Jesus...a quiet crazy trinity. To make matters worse the only time available was 6am on Saturday mornings. Who says yes to that??? Kay said yes, and Jesus said no to inviting anyone else.

Kay and I met every Saturday morning at 6am, rain or shine, while our families slept, on her living room floor from January till May. She always had coffee for me. She was always in her pajamas. And we would sit on her living room floor, and I would open the vault of my life and tell her the things that haunted me, through age old tears. And I would cry about my life, because there were parts of my life that were really really sad. And some Saturdays we would never get to the Bible Study at all, and just sit and talk, but for me I was saying out loud things I had never said before...I was asking for prayer in some of my darkest secrets...I was telling the truth behind the party girl...taking things out of the darkness and blinking in the light of

Christ. Sometimes I would come with a laundry list of things I had to tell her, and Kay would listen and point me to scripture and listen and offer advice and listen and cry with me and listen some more. We worked slowly and painstakingly through, "Breaking Free" by Beth Moore. There were Saturdays where Kay would hold so firmly to the advice and life application in the Bible Study that I would want to shoot her, but I would do what it said because my daughter's life was the cost of me not getting healthy. Grace would never get to have the life she was meant to have if I couldn't become the mother Christ intended me to be…So, I would curse Beth Moore and Kay and Jesus and anyone else who I thought deserved it, and still keep moving forward, unpacking the heaviest baggage and bringing things out of the darkness and into the light. And my baggage was getting lighter. And I was sleeping better. And I was crying more often at real life and not just commercials. I was finding freedom in Christ, and it was just so freeing.

During this time, the Bible became my life line. I did not just read the words, or think they were neat, or think it was just great the way that God would give you just the right words at just the right time…I held on to them with a death grip. His words were living and active and the Bible was alive and offering freedom through Christ Himself. Jesus was speaking to me through words written thousands of years ago. Isaiah 61 was written to me. And I sobbed to read why Jesus came to this earth…He came for people like me. As I read Jeremiah 29:11 with new eyes, and realized it was written to a people who were headed into slavery, and God telling them He knows the plans He has for them…plans to prosper them, plans for good…and they are walking a road to slavery believing this…and it was written for me. As I read about the armor of God and saw that His sword was the Bible, the Word of God, and I knew that I had a weapon to fight darkness in my hand...so thankful that He loved me enough to let me know what to fight this crazy fight with...that all the darkness in my life could be destroyed with Jesus and the word of God...with prayer...with the knowledge that God is good, and He loved me. Jesus loves me. It seemed almost too simple. When the lies crept in about someone stealing my Grace, I would pray, I would go to the Bible and read about who God is...how God is good all the time...how God loves little children...how the angels that watch over children are closest to the face of God...and I would say the name of Jesus out loud. This was so different from my efficient headcounts, and plans of Ninja like action. This was so opposite timing myself to get popsicles or waking up in the middle of the night to do bed checks. This was handing it all over to Jesus and saying, you lead. You show me the next step. You are good, and You so desperately want my freedom that you would die upon a cross just to insure that even in death, I would be free.

The ice was cracking and melting daily and what seemed like a rapid pace. I spent so much time praying and flipping through scripture cards which Kay had made me that it became a reflex action to turn to prayer and scripture. It was not an easy process though because at times, most of the time, I was dealing with the fact that I had become so used to the weight of my baggage, so used to the feel of the ice that letting it go was absolutely painful. I felt naked. I felt unusual. I felt like a different person, but I could not grasp who the heck this person was. One Saturday after having bawled my eyes out on Kay's living room floor, I drove home singing about Jesus at the top of my lungs. I heard His voice so powerful and clear, "Come see who I created you to be..." and I could see a frame that had always existed at my mother's house for as long as I could remember. It had all the school pictures from kindergarten through graduation stacked together with graduation at the front. But if you opened the back of the frame, you could pull out a childhood of annual put on your favorite outfit and smile at the camera. I drove to my mom's house, asked for the frame and headed to my house. I stood frozen in my kitchen. I prayed that God would reveal to me who He created me to be. I opened the back of the frame, and there she was...a little girl in kindergarten. She was wearing a pink Strawberry Shortcake dress with an apron attached to the front. She had straight long, blonde hair and perfectly straight bangs. She had a smile that could light up a room. And she looked innocent. She looked happy. She looked like the girly girl she was...in dance...in dresses...loads of lip gloss...hoards of stuffed animals...this is the little girl God creates. I peeled the first grade picture off the stack, and there she was in a Brownie uniform. Perfect little bob this year, a smile that could light up a room, so sweet and innocent...she looked older, but she looked happy...she looked like a little girl. Then I peeled off second grade, the man in the woods has already ruined everything, and this little girl is so fat. Her grandfather has taken to calling her, "Fat Jack". The smile is there for the pictures, but it doesn't touch her eyes and the difference between the pictures is actually shocking. Then I peeled third grade, and the little girl is gone...her hair is short and unkempt and she is wearing clothes that look like a boys clothes. She is not really smiling. This is the year her teacher would call home to her mother and ask if something was wrong or if something had happened to me because I was way to affectionate with my 3rd grade boyfriend. And somewhere between there and my kitchen I had learned to be really funny and smile with my eyes no matter how I felt inside. Somewhere I had forgotten the girl in kindergarten who was adorable and resigned myself to being someone else...someone a little tougher...someone a little quicker to point out how unattractive she was...someone who trusted no one except herself and adopted a take it or leave it attitude that typically effected all relationships and pushed people away when she felt like she cared too much. Someone who was not worth a hill of beans, was not worth saving, was not worth much at all except a good cup of coffee and a laugh a minute. And Jesus was wrecking it all. Jesus was wrecking all the work I had done to forget the little girl in the picture, and I was that little girl and Jesus loved that little girl so much.

And I literally got on my face that day to pray. I lay on the floor and I asked Jesus what He wanted from me, and why He was murdering me slowly...I yelled at Jesus through my prayers that day and a bucket of tears spilled all over the floor. Tears for the little girl in the picture who I thought had died under all this wreckage, and here she was...she was me...and I was wrestling out the worst part of all...here was Grace. Grace reminded me so much of the little girl in the picture...of the me God created me to be...that I was faced with the little girl I had been torn away from, and I was not going to lose her again. And I felt Jesus saying, "Love her. She is just like you. And love her the way that I would love her...and know every single time you love her till it hurts that I love you till it hurts too. She is your daughter, and you are mine." And it seemed like it might take a miracle, but I could use a miracle so, I decided I was going to love my daughter...hand the fear of all the bad things to Jesus and just love her and enjoy her and talk to her and play with her and cry all the time...I've been a crying mess ever since. And man, did Jesus show me how to love that little girl. I just had to love her the way He loved me...with my whole life.

And we were doing ok. We were getting better. My husband was my rock star (which is way cooler than just being my rock), and he asked all the time how Jesus was healing me and changing me and about the Bible Study with Kay. And he would talk about how he could see the difference. I felt lighter. I felt joy. I felt hopeful. I could barely look at my kids without sobbing because I loved them all so dang much, but man, it felt good to feel it all. It felt good to get choked up. It felt good to need my husband as I walked this road. It felt good to not be strong enough to do it on my own...it honestly felt good to be weak...I had been strong my whole life and weak was nice because that is where Jesus is strong. And He is actually so much better at this whole saving thing than I ever was.

But Jesus wasn't through with me, and this road was a hard road to walk. I had been asked to sit on The Women's Retreat Committee at my church...something I had sworn I would never do. But something happens when you follow Jesus, you may find that you eat your words on occasion...or quite often if you're me. This committee was amazing. It was filled with the most prayerful, Jesus following women I had ever met. Some of my dear friends were in charge, and I was floored by our weekly Wednesday night meetings where decisions were made with the absolute guidance of The Holy Spirit. The retreat would be taught through the Book of Ruth, and we decided to sprinkle throughout the retreat, "Prayer Testimonies". These would be testimonials by women in our church who would speak about prayer in their life over the last year, and how it had changed them. I was in charge of this project, and decided to video some of them for Sunday morning "commercial" snip its, and also during the meal portion of the retreat. The stories were powerful. Again and again I heard women talking about falling at the feet of Jesus in prayer and Him leading them, holding them, speaking to them, comforting them, changing them...and I felt a nudge to share my story. And I quickly plugged my ears. But I should have known better...I should have known that Jesus is not easily quieted. And it was like the story of Grace years ago, but this time it was just a quiet, ongoing, horribly annoying conversation between Jesus and I every single time I prayed. And I wound up on my face again, late one night after everyone was asleep, and I knew what He was asking me and I was so angry because He had already asked for too much. He had asked me to feel, and care, feel hopeful, and do a Bible Study at 6am for Pete's sake...and now He wanted me to tell my story. Twenty nine years of a secret is not an easy topic of conversation. And I might be on a sinking ship, but I was putting up every last ounce of fight. I told Jesus someday I would be strong enough to share my story, but now was just not that time. The next week at our committee meeting, one of the women sharing their prayer testimony had to back out due to scheduling conflicts. The committee felt lead to vote me in to share what I had been praying about over the last year. And I think Jesus was smirking as I sat there in stunned silence.

The first time I shared my story, my true story, was in front of 250 women. It was the largest retreat our church had ever experienced. As the months turned to weeks, Jesus was very specific about a few things I must do before speaking at the retreat. I first had to tell four of my girlfriends the truth I would be speaking at the retreat. My true story was a shocking story, and it was a hard story to tell, but ultimately it is a story of the freedom Christ is offering everyone. He wants us all to be free, and I needed to ask these four girls to pray that my story would not be a story of fear and terror, but a story of the love of Christ who does not just want our outsides to look pretty, but He wants our hearts to be healed. I needed prayer that I would say the words that would lead other women to desire freedom too. I needed more than just Kay and my husband to talk to about this...I needed some girlfriends too. So, we scheduled a night and I spilled my guts in my friend, Joyce's, apartment. Lots of tears. Lots of not making eye contact. Lots of holding onto my chair for dear life...and lots of love from a few girlfriends. I asked them to pray for me to speak only what Jesus asked me to speak, and I asked them to pray for me as I had to tell my mother what I was going to talk about when I took the stage. It was only a ten minute talk, but ten minutes spent sharing a secret that your mother shares is pretty much the scariest ten minutes ever. I prayed for an opportunity to share with her one on one before the retreat. I knew it was unfair to catch her off guard, and I knew she might not be ok with me sharing. I also knew, no matter what her reaction was, I was supposed to share my story and the power of prayer and Jesus to set me free to love and live the life He had created for me. I was prepared for the worst case scenario, and prayed continually that the opportunity would present itself for me to have, at that time, the hardest conversation of my life.

We were at the park, about two weeks before the retreat, and my mom and I were pushing Jake, Jude and Grace on the tire swing. We were laughing and talking and the kids were having a blast. No one else at the park but us. She told me she had just bought her ticket to the retreat, and was super excited to go. I told her I was going to give one of the prayer testimonials. She asked what I was going to speak on. I told her that I was going to talk about the power of Jesus to heal me because I could not love my daughter because I was afraid she would be kidnapped like we had been and I would not be able to save her...And my mom's face got really pail, and she held on to the side of the tire swing and said, "I thought we were all ok. I just thought we were all ok."

"Mom, I am not ok. I have never been ok."

I told her about the Bible Study, about feeling lighter, feeling different. I told her about realizing who God created me to be. I told her all sorts of things through tears, and gulps for air. I told her about Grace. At the end of my monologue she said that she could not attend this retreat and she was sorry. She said that she was proud of me, but she could not do it. And I understood. And I was sad because even though I was 34 years old, I still wanted my mom there to hear me speak.

About a week before the retreat my mom told me she was going to come to the retreat, but not attend on Saturday because that was the day I would speak. The day of the retreat my mom said that she would come for the first half on Saturday and leave right before I spoke. She wanted to be supportive, but did not feel she could listen to the story I was going to share. When Saturday rolled around she sat at my table. We enjoyed every moment of the early morning portion of the retreat, and the worship was powerful. When it was the break before I spoke, I went to the bathroom and prayed some enormous save me prayers, and hurried to my seat. My mom held my hand. She did not leave. She sat in her chair and never took her eyes off of me as I walked to the podium to share the worst thing that had ever happened to me...the story that had filled her with guilt for 29 years...the secret that had torn us all apart and kept us locked together in darkness. It was the bravest thing I had ever seen my mother do.

I opened with a funny story about my girl Grace. Everyone laughed. And then I told the room of women who knew me, knew the story of the party girl made good, knew my kids, and loved my daughter...I told them the truth behind it all. I told them I had been abducted by a stranger when I was 6 years old, and I told them that at 6 years old in the woods behind my apartments I thought I was going to die. I told them I had been so paralyzed by the fear that the same thing would happen to my daughter that I had not been able to love her because loving her and losing her was the most terrifying thing I had ever been faced with. I told about how Jesus was gracious and had given me Anna to pray for me, a husband been who was a rock star, a Bible Study with Kay that had saved me and a Savior who was saving me. He was melting the ice all around my heart and He was saving me. I told them I had spent this year on my face praying at the feet of Jesus for freedom from all of this mess and He was delivering, and I could love my Gracie Girl...And it was out there, and the whole church would know, and I was still breathing. I stepped off the stage with tears streaming down my face to hug after hug, and words of encouragement and women holding my hand telling me they had walked a road like mine. I was free. I wanted to jump up and down and run around my church. And set the prison of merciless lies I had lived in my entire life on fire and sing praises to Jesus as the whole thing burned to the ground. And as I walked to my table, I saw my mother with her glasses off wiping thousands of tears away and she was surrounded by some of the most amazing women in our church telling her it wasn't her fault and that she must have felt guilty for so many years. Hugging her. Standing with her. Putting so much light all over her darkness. And Jesus spoke straight into that moment.

"Your freedom will set other people free too."

As we rolled into summer, with my first year at work behind me, my 6am Bible Study coming to a close and the retreat done and over with, I began to feel finished. Not in a bad way, but just in the way that a project was complete and now let's move on to whatever is next. Way to go. High fives for Jesus. Love having a daughter. Better marriage. Better parent. Better relationship with Jesus. And on to the next horizon. But Jesus isn't in to loose ends. And there was something we had left to discuss, and this discussion would be heated and it would be fierce and filled with grace and mercy and healing, but it would be hard fought and Jesus would win...but I was going to give it every last breath in me because Jesus was not allowed to ask me one question:

"Do you know I was still God and I was still good even in the horribleness of what happened in the woods?"

And the gloves were off. Those were fighting words. How dare my Jesus ask me if I knew He was still God and He was still good when the worst, most terrifying crime against me happened that day. How dare He pretend like He was there. No one was in those woods except for me, my sister and Satan himself. God forgot. God was too busy. I know you are good God, but it is in spite of what happened 29 years ago in the woods behind my apartment. This argument would continue day after day. This was a prayer argument, a faith argument, an I-might-walk-away-at-the-end-of-this argument, but I kept coming back. I was determined to win. Determined to shut my Jesus up by proving to Him that He was only good outside of that event in my life and He better leave my faith walk alone and not make me come up to heaven and give Him a piece of my mind. And I kept coming back. And He asked another question:

"Do you know I was still God and I still loved you on the worst day of your life?"

Oh my goodness gracious. He did not love me on that day. He turned His back on that day. He may love me now, but how did He love me then? What are you asking me Jesus? And the argument would go on, and He would point me to scripture about His love for me…John 3:16, John 4, Matthew 11:28-30, Matthew 18:2-6, Matthew 18:10…And I would think that this was the worst thing ever. But I kept coming back to prove Jesus ridiculous. And He asked the last question for our summer long argument:

"Do you know, the moment you set foot in that woods, I began to work it all out for the good of those who love me?"

And by this time I was tired. June and July had passed in this nauseating argument. And I was losing this fight. Romans 8:28 was just a plain bother, "And we know that in all things God works for the good of those who love him, who have been called according to his purpose." So many things were wrong with this scripture like the word "know", and the words "in all things"…It was just tiring, and Jesus had an answer for everything. Finally, I decided to listen instead of talk. I decided to hear what He had to say. In August, at the very end of a hot Texas summer, God gave me some earth shattering information. I had the story of the woods all wrong. This was not peaceful, Kenny Loggins circa Top Gun Jesus standing with His back to me in the woods that day. This was angry, battlefield Jesus. This was Jesus who was fighting for the physical life of two little girls. Satan had decided to take us off this planet inside that very woods, blankets were on the ground, a plan had been formulated. And Satan is not an idiot; he knew that killing these two little girls would certainly shatter their mother too beyond repair. And Jesus marched straight into those woods, and fought for our life, a real crazy monumental battle. He shielded us. He protected us. He saved us. And at just the right moment, He whispered in my ear, "Run or die." And I ran. And He made sure the wonderful Christian man was working on his car at just the right moment so that the name of Jesus would be spoken over this day, and a prayer of healing would be lifted high to heaven so that He could answer it 29 years later. He was there. He was good. He loved the living daylights out of me, and from the moment my feet landed on the wrong side of the woods, Jesus began to work it all out. Not just for me, but for all of those who love Him and have been called by Him. He had plans for this story of freedom to bring His children to know Him better. He was God in the woods. He was good in the woods. He loved me in the woods. This knowledge was earth shattering. This knowledge was faith shaping. This knowledge changed everything.

If I could look from the vantage point of all I had seen Jesus do in my life just in the past year, if I could look and see how much love and care He had put into this healing, and see all the good it had brought my husband, my daughter, my sons, my mother, my church community...just by trusting Him....just by knowing that He was going to lead me to freedom...then what if I could know in my worst circumstance that God was good, and He loved me and He was working for the good of not just me, but all those who love Him...Because I could see all the good He had done. I could see that He was there because I was still standing. I could see that He loved me. He showed me the picture of the girl He created, and placed her smack in my home. He gave me Grace. And grace was just so unexpected. And it may have taken 29 years for me to come to the knowledge of the love and goodness of God, but this knowledge changed everything. You see, if you say that you believe the sun will rise tomorrow it sounds good enough. But if you say you KNOW the sun will rise tomorrow, you have seen the absolute difference. When we know something we have studied the facts and know it to be truth, we don't worry about things we know because, hey, we know them. Knowing takes the comfort of believing and turns it into a cornerstone of faith. Knowing God is good builds an ark, parts red seas, blows trumpets so walls will come tumbling down and plants your feet firmly in a Jordan River at flood stage.

My shoes were off. My feet were bare. My toes were at the water's edge. I was ready to take a step.

CHAPTER 5

Crossing Jordan Rivers

To know that God was good and loved me and was working all things out for the good of those who know Him, had changed everything. No, I did not look different on the outside, but I felt different on the inside. I felt bolder. I felt stronger. I felt joy filled. I felt peaceful. I felt like I heard the voice of the Almighty better. And I knew He was speaking and guiding; I didn't just hope He was speaking and guiding. I knew it. He had never forgotten me. He had saved me and been there with me every step of the nightmare in the woods, and He would be there every step of every bad day or hard decision to come. His Word was my lifeline, and I couldn't go a day without it. And I was standing with my feet in this new, crazy Jordan River at flood stage, and I was scared to death, and I was totally excited. And all this talk of abundant life and living radically was about to become my everyday life. And there were a couple of major things Jesus would require of me in August 2010 which would seal the deal to change my life. First, my husband would begin working in Houston, TX during the week. He would come home on the weekends. I would tell Jesus from the beginning of this whole crazy experience that He could move us anywhere in the world, but not Houston, TX. I also felt pretty assured there was no way He would move us, because He changed the landscape and scope of my teaching job the beginning of the 2010 school year.

Sometime in the weeks before school started, I heard from my principal, Jennifer Young, that she was creating a "school" inside our high school called, Colt Academy. This special academy would serve the incoming freshmen that were considered, either spoken or unspoken, the "Least Likely to Succeed." They were the kids who had never passed the standardized tests, or who were often in alternative schools due to behavior, or were living in poverty, or working jobs to help support families, or on drugs, or who had given up or who had been given up on by the school system. They were the kids who were least likely to get enough credits to become sophomores. Ms. Young knew these students were easy to identify. Ms. Young knew high school teachers could pick them out by the end of the first grading period. Ms. Young also loved Jesus. And she knew giving up on any kid was not an option. She believed we could build relationships with each of these children, encourage them and love them and help them find their footing to change their lives through education. I was inspired and placed on a team with five other inspired teachers, a couple of assistant principals, and an amazing counselor who were handpicked to change some lives.

We went to special meetings and special trainings before school started. I wondered how I was going to be able to pour into this program and raise three kiddos as a single mom while Corey lived in Houston. And Jesus just worked it all out. When you are working with a team of committed teachers who believe in teaching kids, no matter how hard or how unappreciated their work is, because teaching is what they were designed to do. when your fearless leader is praying for you and will speak words of encouragement into your life, stepping into the Jordan River is still scary, but it feels so refreshing that you come to know there is no other place you want to be than inside His awesome, difficult, exhausting and amazing will. We planned. I prayed. We decorated rooms. We moved my desk to be closer to the Colt Academy classrooms. We were nervous. We were excited. What would I have in common with these kiddos—mid-thirties (or so), middle class Jesus Freak, who only listened to "Jesus Music," living the now oh-so-cleaned-up life?

And then we met our students. There were about 100 of them on the first day of school. The idea was that they would go to classes together and the classes would be smaller; and I, as a special education teacher, would be there to re-teach and assist and co-teach. They were mostly angry to be with us. They were embarrassed. They did not feel like it was fair. And they were hard. They had been either hardened by their lives and circumstances or they had become hardened to the fact that they were "no good" and they had given up on themselves. They were not the smiley, happy freshmen I saw in other places throughout the school. They were the ones who knew too much, had done too much, or had done nothing at all because they had been forgotten years ago at the back of a classroom. And here we were, a team of teachers ready to teach and change lives, lead by a principal who knew Jesus had called us to love, and we were all stuck with each other.

So, when Jesus calls you to put your feet in a Jordan, you have lots of ideas what this amazing miracle journey is going to look and feel like. I had dreams of lives radically transformed in one grading period through this new special school. I had dreams of children becoming National Merit Scholars. I had dreams of kiddos pouring out their love for us, and saying they wanted to renounce their gang memberships or their drug dealing businesses or become star players on the basketball court or football field. I had dreams that looked like made-for-TV movies. And Jesus, He had something bigger. Jesus called me to love. There was no miracle 6-week turnaround. There were no gang renunciations. There were hurting, angry, sometimes unloved kiddos who did not respond all to well to this crazy love in the beginning. Jesus would wake me up early in the morning to pray for them by name. I would drive in to school praying and crying and praying some more. I would pray over the classrooms. I would pray all day at school. And I would smile and love. I would encourage and love. I would pray for the other teachers, too. And I was called to love them big as well. This Jordan River did not contain a trip to Africa or a drive to the inner city. This Jordan River did not require me selling my possessions or living in a tent or passing out pamphlets. (Although, I would have done any of those because that seemed more radical than just loving people.) But loving people that have not been loved in a while or loving people that don't trust love or loving people that don't want to be loved by you...well, it requires a whole bunch of Jesus. And it was hard. And there were days that I was so angry with my students. But I was on a team with amazing teachers who were teaching children to read or do math or actually listen and pass history, I didn't have all of that much to offer, but I had Jesus, and He said to love big.

We would have meetings with our team and say, "These students are hungry." And someone would get food donated. And we would meet and say, "They don't have school supplies." And someone would get school supplies donated. It was unreal. We had all stepped into this unknown adventure together, and it was hard and heavy, but the needs were being met. And the kiddos could see it, too. And my desk became a canvas filled with thank you notes and pictures and drawings. And things were slow to change, but man the changes were worth the wait. It was inspiring some days and draining others. My thoughts were filled with *This kid is never going to change* as much as they were filled with *Even if nothing changes we have to know we tried*. And there were tears and hugs in the hallway. And there were long, patient, "I wouldn't push you so hard if I didn't love you" meetings on the steps of the school. There were notes written to our students from the principal as they accomplished tiny victories, and they would keep those notes tucked into their folders because it had been way too long since a note like that had been written. There were phone calls and meetings with parents. There were emails from other teachers in the building who were getting on board with changing lives. There were boundaries crossed and reestablished. And no matter what, Jesus said to love. And I began to feel like a mom to the children. And I wanted to fight for them like I would fight for my own. And there was nothing I wouldn't do for them. And this was not coming from me. It was coming from Jesus. Because I was raising three kiddos by myself and working full time and running to sports and dance and PTA, and I was busy trying to keep my marriage intact with a man I only saw on the weekends. And Jesus just kept saying to love.

The revelation was enormous when it came. It literally was so huge that I was almost knocked over in the hallway. I was having a motivational-speech-type conversation with one of the girls in our program. I was telling her she could change her life and it would be hard and how much I loved her and how much Jesus loved her, and she was crying, and I was crying. And in that moment, Jesus whispered, "this is who you would have become if your mom had not become a Christian. This is who you would have become if Mac had not become your step dad. This is who you would have become if you had stayed right where you were all those years ago. You, Jackie Hooks, are looking in a mirror." All of a sudden, I knew this girl differently. I knew her heartache and need and desperation to be loved. I knew it was far easier to be the wild girl than it ever was to be the girl who changed. And I realized Jesus had placed me right there, in this group of kiddos, because I knew where they were coming from: the place of overlooked and forgotten and not good enough and giving up and giving in and "where is this Jesus if He isn't saving me." And I realized that this crazy love Jesus was causing me to have for these students—who were not always nice to me, who were willing to make fun of me, who would try to take advantage of me, who were horrible to each other, who made astonishing choices, and who would have a ticket to a new life in their hands and tear it up and throw it all away—was His love, and I was to be part of His plan to pour it all over their lives. And this inspiring job became a daily Jordan River. And it was worth every tear shed because the Promise Land we were trying to reach belonged to Jesus' precious children. I began to love them with my life.

This was about healing. This was about trusting. This was about seeing all the effort Jesus had put into me and all the people He had put in my path as I witnessed all He was willing to do for every single one of my students. Now, they could choose to accept His love and help or not, but He never stopped being there. Not once. And in the midst of all of this love for all of these children was Kalee. Kalee was a fellow teacher on the team. She was young and beautiful, wickedly smart with an incredible sense of humor. She and I got along so fabulously it was ridiculous, and being paired with her was way too much fun. She was passionate about the students and loved them so fiercely. She worked hard and received impressive results. We would have long talks about the students and what needed to be done for them. We would be angry together or disappointed together or so unbearably sad together as students chose to leave our program due to drug use or gangs or poor choices. And Kalee and I talked about Jesus all the time, and religion and God and church. But Kalee was not a believer. Kalee believed in anything and everything. And there was this other conversation Jesus kept having with me. He told me every day that I would love her and listen and never judge her. She was one of the most loving and giving people I had ever met, but she was without Jesus. Some days I would catch a glimpse of how amazing her life would be if she had Jesus. He would move mountains through her. And Jesus said every day, "Love. Listen. Encourage. Live life with her. And pray. Never judge." And, oh my goodness, I prayed y'all. And I loved. And a friendship grew and grew between two girls. One who was doing what Jesus had called her to do and the other who was simply doing the right thing. And the kiddos loved us both. And Jesus loved us both. And there were days when I thought it was incredible that Jesus would have me walking through my first Jordan River with a girl who did not realize her feet were planted on a path where He had parted the water for her.

It was crazy, all the things Jesus did with that one Jordan River. All the lives He spent time changing each day. Some days it was just about food and feeding the hungry. Some days it was about me receiving a bag of teenage boy/girl clothes and being able to share that with a student who didn't have any. Some days it was about just offering hugs and love and encouragement. He used my hands and feet so much that I thought they would fall off. And then, when I was beyond tired, He would use someone in *my* life. This came in the form of a wonderful counselor at the school, who worked with our kids and, in turn, would put me back together on occasion. This came in the form of amazing coworkers all around where my desk was located. We laughed. We cried. We were fighting the good fight together. This came in the form of my girlfriends from church who would call or text or check in on me and my crazy life. This came in the form of encouragement from all of my family, not just the ones who understood Jesus' call on my life, but also the ones who didn't understand yet totally supported me anyway, because changing the lives of forgotten kiddos spoke to everyone. It was a meeting place for everyone. It was a place where we could see each other's hearts. It was a place where we became a team, not just those of us teaching at Arlington High School, but all around the city and my church and my family. Jesus was shining His light all over.

That spring semester, as we struggled at times to keep the momentum alive at school, life was still churning away in my home too. My husband was nearing what I thought would be the end of his stent in Houston. He was almost home again. He was almost back to living all the time in our world. When he was down to one remaining week of the back-and-forth journey to Houston, I was overjoyed. I saw life getting back to normal. I saw us getting back to a routine. I saw everything fitting into this new, perfect package of me and my awesomely rewarding job with Corey back in town and following Jesus into any Jordan River...I just didn't know that Jesus' plans sometimes don't fit into my prepaid packages. And my plans sometimes look totally different than Jesus' plans. When I told Corey about how excited I was to have him back home, he told me he really felt like Jesus was calling our family to Houston. You could have heard a pin drop. You could not have dropped a bigger bomb in my lap. You could have looked into our kitchen and seen a woman who was being rocked to the core. And the same questions popped up: *Jesus, do I know you are good? Jesus, do I know you love me? Jesus, do I know you are working all things out for the good of those who love you?* I already knew the answer. YES. And with that YES, no matter how cold and uncomfortable and terrifying, my feet had to go into a new Jordan River. I knew Jesus was good in the nightmare of my life. How could I not trust that He would be good and loving and would work all things out in a move to Houston? Did I like this new plan? No. Did I know Jesus was up to something amazing? Yes. Was putting my feet into this Jordan River going to be easy? No. Did I know the rewards of following Him into the water at flood stage? Yes.

I would have to go back to what I knew about Jesus sometimes every hour. I would have to revisit that Jesus was good and loved me and had an amazing plan for my life over and over. And this plan was going to be in Houston. And any time I doubted, someone came along to remind me that I was supposed to move with my husband. On occasion I concocted my own plans, like moving in with my mom and staying and working for one more year. I would tell Jesus I knew He would never take me away from this job and these kids I loved. I would tell Him I knew He would not take my children away from their grandparents. I would tell Him that I knew He would not place my feet in one Jordan River to take me out of it and plant my feet in another. And in the middle of me telling Jesus all the things I knew about His plan, He reminded me that He saw me through the woods and would see me through this move. As crazy as it sounds, trusting His voice in my husband's ears was one of the most difficult adventures of my life. And He placed about 9 million women in my life to remind me how important it was for me to go with my husband to Houston, not just for Corey's career, but for our marriage too. Were we in another rough patch? No. But if I didn't go we would be. So, I prepared to leave. I planned out what moving would look like, and I began to take off my shoes to feel the water rush over my feet as I stepped into this next Jordan River. However, Jesus was not letting my plan unfold in the way I had anticipated.

I have always been a fan of the "fade." I have always been a fan of letting things die out so the pain is far less when you leave or move on or have to go. I like my heart to be protected. (This is not necessarily a good thing.) And during this move Jesus was very clear with me: I would not fade from people's lives at all. I would still give 158 percent to my students, my friends, my family, my church, and my coworkers when it came to my heart and how much I poured into them. And it would hurt when I left, but the pain would be worth the relationships and memories I had made in His name. He gave me this crazy notion of Jesus Friends, and how different they were than regular friendships. And in the middle of living alone, planning to move, teaching students that I loved more than I could have ever imagined, and juggling my own three children I was asked to lead our church women's retreat with the idea of these Jesus Friendships at the forefront. It was crazy. As I was preparing to teach others, Jesus was teaching me all the things I needed to not just love the women I was leaving in a big way, but to prepare me for a season of having to make new friends too. And so my plans to fade were thwarted and I dug in to love 'til the bitter end, and then love some more.

I honestly expected after my freedom in the name of Jesus and healing that I would get to actually go somewhere on a mission trip. I thought maybe I would resume my work at Mission Arlington. Jesus had this daily plan though. Jesus had a plan to live radically every day, not just for special events. He had this plan that included loving people even when it hurt, and then loving them some more. Jesus said that I would act like Him even when it didn't seem worth it. Jesus said that I would be filled with His joy and not have any other agenda except to do exactly what He said, go exactly where He was leading, and love everyone everywhere along the way. And this Jordan River became THESE Jordan Rivers. There was the Jordan River I was crossing for the students I was teaching. There was the Jordan River I was crossing as I prepared to move to Houston. There was the Jordan River I was crossing with Kalee as our relationship continued, and our conversations continued, and I prayed for her daily. And there was the Jordan River I crossed, sometimes hourly, to trust Jesus with my own children and stand fearlessly knowing that Jesus loved them far more than I ever could. Sometimes it felt like the hardest part of walking through these Jordan Rivers was not the walking so much as the belief that you were still walking them whenever you had a setback. If I had a misstep and didn't love like Jesus, because I am human and I am not actually Jesus, Satan was right there to tell me I had not changed. If I felt full of fear surrounding my Grace, and pulled her into the house all of a sudden or needed to go walk around the house at night to count heads in beds, Satan was right there to remind me that I had not really been set free. If I spent a day pulling back from my Jesus Friends to protect myself from the pain of moving, Satan was right there to point out that I could never stay inside the will of God. These Jordan Rivers were not an easy hike. They were daily and different than I ever expected. I had to dig deep inside His word to hear His voice each day. And as I prepared for the upcoming women's retreat, the account of Mary and Elizabeth in Luke Chapter 1 became my lifeline.

As I read about this friendship between these two women, Jesus began to show me how He had used the friendships in my life to lead me to Him. He began to show me how He had been there in my everyday from the very beginning of my crazy faith journey that began in 2005. I could see Him weaving His love for me through my daily life, and not just inside my family, although He was definetly there, but inside my playgroup, my Thursday night women's Bible Study, my text messages at just the right time, and the women who would cheer me on as I was freed from years of chains by the hands of my almighty savior. He had placed these women in my life just like He had placed Elizabeth in Mary's life, and He was wanting to place this kind of love in everyone's life. And I began to realize, as a Christ Follower, that His love pouring out of me daily was the most important work I would ever do on this earth. This love, this friendship, this abundant life was for everyone. And so everyone was to receive it. And I failed all the time. Especially when it came to people who hurt me, my kids, or my husband; but Jesus was clear, and this love was for them too. This love seemed to move mountains. This love seemed to unite Christians to non-Christians. This love seemed to build bridges. And this love made me stronger because this love did not come from me. This love came from Jesus, and just when I thought I didn't have any more love to give, Jesus gave more to me and I was able to give a little more too.

Knowing the goodness of God made my faith walk so much clearer. I came to understand that the little "nudges" I had always felt in the moment were actually huge, supernatural pushes. I began to understand that when someone unexpectedly leapt into my mind it was not random. I needed to pray for that person and then tell them so. I began to realize when I sensed the need to give a student a hug, it was absolutely the right time to do so. When I began to feel the need to call my husband and tell him I loved him, he may need to hear it more than I realized. Texts, phone calls, facebook messages, hugs, telling someone they look great, encouraging someone, all of these things could be used by Jesus to help people continue to walk in their own Jordan River. And I no longer felt afraid of people disagreeing with my faith. I had plenty of people in my life who did not believe in Jesus at all, or who didn't believe in "organized religion," or who believed in a little bit of everything. This used to make me feel like I had to defend myself, but I came to realize I could just listen or just talk or just love bigger than all our differences, and so our differences didn't matter anymore. My students began to say that they liked "My Jesus." My Jesus was the real Jesus. He just felt so different inside of me when I chose to listen to Him instead of all the things people said about Him. Jesus said love. And loving was the hardest thing I could think of most times, but it made the most difference hands down.

Not everything was tied up in a big pink bow. The drive back and forth to Houston was really beginning to wear on Corey and cause tension at home. My desire to stay right where I was, in Arlington, with my students and my family grew stronger each day, and I would be a liar if I didn't say I was still pleading with Jesus to work it all out to fit my plans. The need to pull back and fade was stronger than ever too. But as the school year neared the end, some people began to speak truth into my life. First, one of the ladies on the retreat committee, who was older than me, had heard me talk here and there about maybe staying and teaching one more year because "Jesus would never truly make me leave a place I loved so much." She took me to lunch one day and let me know that my home was already in Houston. My husband lived there, so my home was there because we were supposed to be together. There was no way, for sure, that he was calling me to my job over my husband. It was time for me to wrap my head around what I already knew, if Jesus was calling me away from what amazing work He was doing at Arlington High School, then clearly there was more work to be done somewhere else. And in the midst of all the crazy and the standardized testing and the worry and whatnot, Jesus asked me to write. I had not written anything more than a thank you note or an email since I began dating Corey. Over a decade had past. And what was Jesus asking of me in the middle of asking so much of my heart?

The lifeline that had always kept me afloat was my writing, and now instead of writing for myself, I was writing for Jesus...out of this crazy obedience simple because He told me to write. And all I knew was I was about to write about Jesus and for Jesus because Jesus was good.

I ended up writing a Bible Study called, *Different Here*. It was about how friendships are supposed to be different among women inside The Body of Christ. It seemed like such a simple concept, and so obvious, but as I wrote, I realized how much Jesus had protected me from inside the world of female friendships. I realized since I was so desperate to understand Jesus, I had let Jesus pick my friends. And many of us were the least likely friends, but we had Jesus in common, and to me that made all the difference. Jesus allowed my Jesus Friends to love me and never leave me in a way I had never experienced. They prayed for me every step of my journey. They prayed for my kids, my parents (all four of them), my sisters, my home, my marriage, my finances, my students, my move, my heart, my everything. He gave me friends who didn't judge me but who called me on the carpet when I needed to hear it. He gave me girlfriends who weren't perfect but who were at least honest with their struggles. He gave me people to pray with in a way I had never prayed before. And the Bible Study that poured out of my soul felt like a love letter from Jesus pointing to all the ways He had carried me during my first Jordan Rivers through the Jesus Friends He had blessed me with at just the right time. He was there reminding me He had been there all along, that He would be there for the next step of my journey, and that all the prayers I had prayed throughout the halls of Arlington High School for my students and for Kalee were heard by the most amazing and mighty king. And Jesus was working all those rivers out for good too. And as I wrote, I saw how He had worked it out for me in every detail of every friendship, giving me all the love He needed me to know was from Him. There was praise and worship inside the pain and fear of crossing my Jordan Rivers that year. And even though the Promised Land on the other side held so much unknown, I knew Jesus was mapping it all out. And how could I say no to that?

The school year came to a close and the majority of students we taught became sophomores. It wasn't pretty, but for most we had made it. As teachers we were thankful and tired, and I was saying goodbye to a job I loved and people who I loved working with every single day. I had students I feared I would never see again who I knew would hold a piece of my soul forever. My students had changed me forever. They were the faces of hardship and pain. They were the faces of those who had been given up on and who had learned to give up on themselves. They had not made loving them easy, yet Jesus never let me do anything but love them. And this love for people who told you they didn't want your love or didn't love you back or didn't even like you...well, it changed things. Because in the end, Jesus knew what He was talking about when He called us to love our neighbor. Love changes everything. Love changes the landscape. Love changes raging rivers into dry ground because your desire is so tremendous to see the ones you love on the other side. I would see their faces from time to time and know I needed to pray for them and look back on the first Jordan River I willingly stepped into because of Jesus' prompting. Sure, there had been other Jordan Rivers before this year, but I had just been drug across those. Making it to the other side was God dragging a girl kicking and screaming. These Jordan Rivers were about me walking with God, hearing His voice, and walking some more.

Days before school let out, I sat in Kalee's classroom. It was empty, outside of her and I and Jesus, and I told her my whole Jesus Story of hurt and healing and freedom in Christ. I told her she had so many questions, but she just really needed Jesus. And I cried. I cried because I knew that I would move from Arlington and she was not a Christ Follower and she might never be and my job had been to love and plant seeds and that was it. And now my job would be to love from outside of Houston, in a city called Katy. Having to trust Jesus, that He would place others in her life to continue to point her to Him, was one of the hardest things I have ever done. But, again, Jesus is big and He had a mighty mighty plan. This Jordan River I had crossed with Kalee taught me to love with abandon and expect nothing in return. I had loved her and been my same Jesus-loving self in front of her, and nothing had changed except that we were really good friends. Did I want her to breakdown that day in her classroom and pray to have Jesus as her Lord and Savior? Sure. But I believe Jesus has a special place in His heart for the strong-willed, and there was no girl I knew with more strength and will as Kalee. And Jesus said to never stop praying and never stop believing that He would have His hand all over her life, but it would be on His time and not mine.

I spent my last summer in Arlington, TX, the place where I had grown up, the place where my life had fallen apart and the place where Jesus had put it all back together, teaching the Bible Study I had written to the girls I had written about. Every Tuesday night we gathered and talked about how friendships inside The Body of Christ were supposed to look and feel and be different. We talked about aches that had cut to the core and friendships that had been revived by Christ alone. We laughed and cried. We were able to see how Jesus had orchestrated some powerful friendships and given us powerful women to walk shoulder to shoulder with in His name. And Jesus would whisper in my ear, *you are going to love them with 150 percent even as you prepare to give 150 percent to the friends I will bless you with in Katy.* And as my heart wanted to hide and hold my hands up at the thought of leaving some of the friends who had carried me through and prayed me through all of my Jordan Rivers, Jesus would always say, you can walk shoulder to shoulder with these girls even if you don't see them for years. Trusting that these friendships would remain, even when time and distance had done their duty, seemed near impossible, but I knew He was good and would be true to his word. I knew He loved me. I knew He was working all things out for me and for those around me.

And my faith grew stronger as I prepared to leave and trusted Him with my next Jordan River. I was not perfect, but I was being perfected. I was not amazing, but I was amazed at all Jesus could do when I trusted Him alone and simply knew, as a fact, his goodness and love and power. His plans were always good. My husband would pray about where we were supposed to live in this new city neither of us knew anything about except for the fact that everyone kept telling us to move there. Corey would pray and come back with the square footage he felt like God was calling us to move into. Each time of prayer would result in less square footage until we were finally planning to move into a house smaller than the first house we had lived in, and barely bigger than the apartment he had rented for 6 months. We had to get rid of all sorts of furniture just to fit in the new house. Some things we were allowed to sell. Other things Jesus placed on our heart to give away. We gave away couches, beds, desks, dishes, a piano, Christmas decorations, and so much more. And as God took so many things away before we left Arlington, He gave us the promise that we would be ok in Katy. He gave us peace as we started the new leg of our life. He gave us each other and three beautiful children.

We officially moved to Katy the last week of July 2011. It was a move filled with tears, and prayers that we would move back soon. We left an amazing church home, a school we loved, a familiar life filled with family and comfort. We left behind everything we knew with the belief that God knew better. And God was God, and things began to fall into place. Because of the size of our house, and the decision to live beneath our means, I was able to stay home for the next year with Grace. There was no pre-school for Grace her last year before kindergarten. There was just me and the daughter who had changed my life hanging out together. It was the best present Jesus could have given me. My son, Jake, had left first grade with the heartbreak of being bullied on a daily basis. He was not punched or hurt or threatened, he was simply ignored for 8 hours a day. When he would try to speak to someone throughout the day, no one would speak to him. He was terrified to start a new school. He was literally shaking walking in to the first day of 2nd grade in a new city. The moment his classroom door swung open, we were greeted by a wave of peace. He would have the sweetest class that year. I would tell Corey, if I had seen a picture of what Jesus had in store for Jake, I would have put him on my back and walked to Katy just to get there for my boy. It was beyond our expectations. And Jude, his love of music began to blossom so completely in a church we went to that first year. You could sit back some days and watch Jesus at work in my family's life. You could see Him working all things out for good in each of our lives. Jesus is big y'all.

From the "shores" of Katy, TX I could stand and look back across my Jordan Rivers. I could look back and see me trying to swim on dry land. I could see me kicking and screaming and throwing fits. I could see me begging Jesus to do His work more like me. I could see myself doubting every step. I could see Him placing His arm around my shaking shoulders and letting me lean on Him. I could see Him placing friends, students, and colleagues all around me to cheer me on as I took baby steps of faith. I could see my husband growing into the man who would trust a Jordan River because Jesus would always clear the water. I saw my family becoming a tight knit unit relying on Jesus more than we relied on our own understanding. It was incredible to see what God could do with our path when we told Him we would really follow Him. And nothing was nice and neat and tied up in a pretty bow, but life was good. And we knew there were more Jordan Rivers coming. So, we took of our shoes and got ready for some Jesus adventure. We were just totally wrong about the adventure ahead.

CHAPTER 6

Pruning Hooks

We had lived in Katy for almost a year. God had been faithful. We had crossed what felt like an enormous Jordan River and sat on the other side in the sprawling, immaculately master-planned community with exemplary schools everywhere. Sometimes it felt like the Promise Land; sometimes it felt like the Stepford Wives. Either way, we were sitting on the shores with new friends. And sometimes that is all you need.

God had brought me to a table in a Bible Study filled with amazing women who would become my lifeline. He had given me friends to pray with and friends for my kids too. He had given me two friends to "walk" to school with each day (I actually parked my car and walked up to the building), and I had seen Him hand me blessing after blessing and treasures amidst the pain of leaving my home. I had stayed home with Grace for her last year before school, and I had watched Jesus heal a chasm of pain between my little girl and me. All of the distance I had placed between us was squished out with snuggles in the afternoon, watching some kid movie, just Grace and me at home, while the rest of the world went to school. It was a good first year in a hard place.

During that time, Kalee, my friend I taught with and lived life with and prayed for daily, stopped wrestling and became a Christian. Her transformation would be so impactful in my life. She would step into Christianity with this intense excitement and need to know His will in her life. She read the

Bible like it was water and refreshed my soul with all her questions. She had her live-in boyfriend move out and called off their engagement.

Kalee loved her neighbor bigger than I had seen anyone ever love their neighbor. She continued to build relationships with my former students and offered me the opportunity to still speak into their lives from hours away. Her faith was challenging to me. It was so real and so raw, and I had to wonder if my life looked much different than other people's lives here in Katy. Was I wrestling anything out with Jesus? Was I just bee bopping along, getting just radical enough to be more radical than the girls I saw on Sunday mornings? Was I listening? Or had I fallen asleep just enough to not worry about my faith much anymore? The fire burning bright in Kalee's new walk with Jesus was sending sparks over into my tired walk and waking me up just enough.

During that first year in Katy, Texas, God also asked me to start writing a blog. I was so super annoyed. Everyone had a blog, and here I was starting a blog in my late thirties. Who did God think I was anyway? I didn't have time to write. And who would read it? And if people did read it then that seemed terrible too. I was not excited about this blog. But God was persistent, and I felt compelled and convicted and certain that no one would read it much.

The blog would be called "Undignified," constructed after the verse that seemed to sum up my entire life: And I will become even more undignified than this, and I will be humiliated in my own eyes. (2 Samuel 6:22) If this truly was my life's verse, then I would prove how undignified I was willing to become by writing this blog the way Jesus told me to. From the beginning, my husband was my biggest fan. He told me how great every post was and gave me the courage to write and put stuff on the Internet for anyone to read.

Before I left Arlington, I had promised a dear friend that someday, somehow I would seek a counselor to help me shore up all the work Jesus and I had done together. I found my counselor, Amy McGown. I sat in her office on the deepest couch and told her I had spent my life being angry. And now I felt like I was sad, for the first time ever, as I was watching Grace grow. I was sad for all the years that were stolen from me. I was sad for all the innocence lost. I was sad, and sad was new, and there was a part of me that was afraid this sadness was going to take me under, and I might sit on her couch forever and never get up. Amy walked me into my sadness. She walked me there and said that I should be sad. She said my life had been sad and terrifying in some parts and that sadness and fear made perfect sense. She said that I was a totally normal girl reacting to totally abnormal situations. And she said that Jesus and I had done a ton of good work. And from there, Amy and Jesus and I did a little more work to stand securely in His victory.

It was the spring of 2012 where I learned about the targets Satan had placed on my back from the very beginning. We traced God's fingerprints all over my journey, and I could see the battle raging from the distance of thirty years. Amy listened. I cried some. I cussed a lot. Amy pointed toward healing. Amy pointed toward Jesus. Amy gave me permission to feel everything I had felt for so long, and then she gave me permission to give my story to Jesus. We had claimed it back from Satan, and I had held it in trembling hands for the last few years, and it was finally time to hand it to Jesus and let Him do whatever He needed to do with it. But before Jesus could own it, one man had to know my life story: my dad, who I had always held at arms length; my dad, who only knew me as super happy or completely absent—never angry, never sad, just happy and easy and funny. I told Amy I thought he would say nothing at all or act like it was no big deal. Those were my two greatest fears. I mean, what if I told him and my dad, the person that you need to save you and protect you, changed the subject and asked me how the kids were doing? What if he said that he was real sorry and he was busy and he had to go? I was convinced one of these things would happen, and I played out those scenarios with Amy. And we prepared for my phone call. And I prayed like I was losing my mind.

The day I called my dad, there was no one else at my home. I was standing in my kitchen, and as he answered the phone I walked into the laundry room. As we were going through the usual small talk, which occurs at the beginning of any conversation, I sat on the floor. And as I plunged into the words, "I have to tell you something," I turned off the lights. I needed to be so small. I needed to feel so safe. I needed no one to see me or hear me; and even though no one was home, the floor of the dark laundry room was the only place I could find to step into the light. Maybe it was my last ditch effort to stay in the dark. The dark had been where I hung out my whole life with my secret, and now the last person who should have known was going to know, and there would be no shred of darkness anymore.

The words started slowly, and I had to force myself to breathe. And then they were tumbling out of me like a long overdue waterfall, like a flood. And I was telling about the man in the woods and I was telling about the terror and I was telling about the police and I was telling that they never caught him. I was crying. I was letting tears roll all down my face, and I could see the little girl in me so lost, and I was so sad because her story was so sad, and there was silence on the other end of the line. I couldn't break the silence. I prepared myself for my dad to change the subject. I prepared myself for him to make light of it. And when he finally spoke he said these words: "Jackie. What you just told me changes everything. It changes everything. And Jackie, what you just told me changes nothing at all. You are still my beautiful little girl who is smart and funny, and I love you so much. I always have. I just wish this hadn't happened." And in those words I heard the voice of Jesus pouring all over me, wrapping me up and telling me that he loved me so much through the father He gave me here on earth. Satan had just gotten in the way and messed it up for a long, long time. Now, here we all were with the truth, and it was setting us all free. And then we cried. And I cried really, really, really hard. And I told him that he was going to have a million and five questions over the next few weeks and months, and the door to this conversation was always open. I hung up the phone, and I felt like I could breathe differently. I felt a joy that I think had been waiting for me my entire life. And I sat on that laundry room floor for a while longer, and then said goodbye to the darkness and shame forever.

As that first year was coming to a close and summer was upon us, I prepared to go back to teaching. Grace was headed to kindergarten, and it made absolute sense for me to return to work. I was excited about the thought. I was excited about the income, and I figured life would go on as normal. I felt like I had stepped out of my comfort zone in a myriad of ways over the last year. I had moved for goodness sake, I had served the homeless, I had given to people who were in need, and I had loved big. I had read the book of James and felt wholly convicted by every sentence. I had led a Bible study group in my neighborhood. I had taught a fantastic group of kids at Vacation Bible School. I had finally gone to counseling and shared my secret with my dad. I had done well in my eyes as a Christian, and now it was time to go back to work and love on the people and students I would meet at a new high school. In my opinion, life would fall into place and really get back to normal. And I needed some normal. God, I was pretty certain, would answer all of our needs and worries through one job. This was going to be a great year.

It happened one night while I was watching Grace in her dance class. I was staring through the window as my precious baby danced and goofed off on a Wednesday night in the summer. I was thinking how happy I was she was my youngest because I would pour into her. She was the perfect baby of the family, and our family was so complete. The thought that landed in my head next was not my own: *I'm pregnant.*

I tried to shake the thought, but it came back again and again. And by the time I was driving home from dance class, I felt like I was having an internal shouting match with myself. Corey and I put the kids to bed that night, and after they were all asleep I told him that I knew I was crazy, and I hoped I was crazy, but I kept thinking that I was pregnant. He got up , went to the store, and came back with three pregnancy tests.

He thought I was crazy too. There was no way. There was just no way. And we didn't want another baby. We were happy with what we already had, and our hearts had really been closed to having another baby in our house. I mean, I didn't even like to hold babies. I didn't think infants smelled "so good."

I just wasn't a big fan. So, this was silly. This was me being paranoid.

Three positive pregnancy tests later and we were faced with some facts: (1) Yes, we were pregnant. (2) No, we did not want another baby. (3) By the sound of our silence, we had no idea what to do about it. We sat and stared at a TV screen, aimlessly trying to find excitement down deep and making some lame remarks about how this would be ok. They sounded more like questions than statements. I felt like I was drowning, and I began to ask God why He would give me another baby when I was finished having babies. Why would He even consider me as an option for a mom? I was older. I was happy right where I was. I was not interested in adding another person to an already crowded little home. I was not interested in gaining weight. Had He not noticed how hard I was working to take off the "baby weight" I had kept on for the past five years from being pregnant with Grace? And these conversations would rage on relentlessly for the next three months.

There would be days I was excited. There would be days I was utterly depressed. Ultimately, I just really felt like I had been handed a stick of butter at the end of a marathon. Functional? Sure. Anyone can use butter, and it is great at just about any meal. Who doesn't love butter? But at the end of a marathon? Well, no one wants butter then. I would read everything I could in the Bible about how God feels about children, and man oh man, He really seemed to like them. He said they are our reward. He said we should be like them. He said they have the right type of faith. But I had just finished running a marathon over the last several years, and a baby was not what I was looking forward to at the end of it...at all.

I was completely baffled by God's reward system. And since I didn't understand His rewards, well, maybe I didn't understand what He and I were doing in the first place. And that summer of 2012 I began to ask God what He wanted with my life. I began to ask Him what His plans were for my life. I began to ask Him if I had missed the point. And it was the scariest question I had ever asked God. His answer would blow down the doors of my soul.

God began to say to me over and over when I prayed that He was not the God of small talk. There were things He had told me to do, and I had not done them. He began to remind me that He does not speak idle words to our heart, and He does not push us and pull us and nudge us to do things just so we can talk about them a lot and never set foot on His path. And He began to lay out things I had not done for Him. So, in August of 2012 I knew beyond a shadow of a doubt I was supposed to go tour a private school in Houston's impoverished Third Ward. He had told me to do it nearly a year before when I had heard a woman give a speech about the school saying they could always use volunteers. And I had simply said, "No." A Lot.

I went and toured the school. I drove to a neighborhood like nothing I had ever seen before with a good friend who had volunteered there for the past year. We prayed during the drive. And honestly, I just figured I would tutor at the school. I mean, I wasn't going back to teaching this year, because no one wants to hire the pregnant teacher. Needless to say, I had some unexpected time on my hands. Clearly, I would tutor the forty kids who needed extra help, and I would bring glory to God. It would be simple. And then I toured the school.

In the heart of a crime-infested neighborhood like so many in Houston, I walked into a building which looked similar to others around the area. Nothing special. Nothing different—until you walked in those doors. And there you met Jesus. Generation One Academy was well hidden in its urban landscape. But that was just the outside. I walked into joy, pure joy, on the faces of children wearing dirty uniforms. I walked into classrooms, with little room and even less resources, where children were learning. These kids were not just learning how to read and write; they were learning that they were loved, and it showed. Joy was everywhere. Hugs were around every corner. I could not stop crying. I could not stop praising Jesus over the light He was shining in such a dark, dark place. He was drawing the students into His light, and you could see how much they loved standing in it. They were drinking His love in, and while I walked the halls and heard their class creeds and received 292 hugs, I could here Jesus saying this was where He was...this was where He hung out.

I went home that afternoon, ready. I was ready to get down to that school and do some tutoring. I was ready to get down there maybe twice a month. I might even go more if Jesus asked me to, and who knew what would happen then. I was going to make Jesus so proud. I lay on my floor praying, basically a power point presentation type prayer, telling Jesus all that I would do for Him. I told Him about the tutoring. I told Him that I might even help identify some of the kids with special needs. I told Him that I would help the school access resources in the community for kids with special needs. I showed Jesus frame after frame of my presentation, and it was a darn good presentation. At the end of my prayer, I could feel Him say that I was not listening. I was just talking. I was standing at the foot of the cross talking at Jesus.

And so I listened. And as He led me all through Matthew 25, He kept saying to feed His children. I decided Jesus had officially gone crazy. How did He expect this family to feed a school? We were working hard to pay off the debt we had accrued by living beyond our income. We were a two-income family existing on one income. We were adding a baby to the mix too. Had He not seen our life lately? Had He not seen the man I was married to who kept our budget balanced to the penny? This could never happen. And with these thoughts I argued with Jesus for a week solid. Anytime I would hear His voice creep in about feeding the students at Generation One, I would remind Him that He had gotten the wrong girl. He would gently begin to say over and over again that my job was to obey. I would protest. He would lead me to His word. I couldn't "un-know" now that this group of kiddos existed. I couldn't "un-know" that this school spent tens of thousands of dollars feeding them. I knew where the least of these were,God had taken me to them, and I could not just walk away. God let me know that if I said yes, He would take care of the rest.

As I snuck closer to obedience, I began to ask Jesus for His plan. He promised an army of women ready to make healthy sack lunches with the students' names on each of them and with scripture inside each bag. He promised He would find every member of this rag tag army, and all I had to do was trust Him. Even my husband was on board. Corey said that if I felt God telling me to feed a school, then I better say yes and feed them. And I began to pray non-stop about this yes, which I was sure was on the horizon. I began to ask for help and for Jesus to reveal to me where this help would come from. I scheduled a meeting with the school, and then prayed help would arrive soon.

On a Tuesday night, during my son, Jake's, football practice, I asked about the sack lunches and told the ladies around me about the school. They all seemed excited. They all said they would help. I told them I had a meeting with the school, and one of the moms, Jody, asked me if I knew what questions to ask the school. I had not even considered coming to this leap of faith meeting prepared with questions, and so, I knew in that very moment God had led me straight to the help I had been praying for.

Jody and I would go to lunch, and she would give me a list of practical questions to ask the school—the first question being: did they want this help to begin with. And Jody became the logic to my emotion with that one question. And with her help to prepare, and 500 pounds of prayer, I was ready for some radical faith.

I cried my way through the meeting with the school. My hands shook as I showed them the scriptures God had sent that led me on this crazy journey. I said that when God asked for my yes, He reminded me how He had asked me to tour the school almost a year prior and that my no had cost them thousands upon thousands. I sat there ashamed of the lack of faith I had shown before when I thought I was being such a good Christian. I sat there embarrassed to sit across from this woman who had lived out a faith so big that she had left her job in South Carolina to move to a ghetto in Houston, Texas, because she had heard the call of her Savior. I sat there with all my excuses burnt down to the ground. It was the most humbling experience of my life.

They were kind. They were shocked. They would have to meet with their board. But they had believed in the beginning, a little over a year ago when they had opened the school, God would send someone to bring free meals, and here I was, just a little over a year late.

The first free, healthy, sack lunches with the students' names on them and scripture inside were served on October 18th. Jody and I delivered them. As we handed out the lunches in the classrooms, you would have thought we brought Christmas with us. The kids were so excited. They wanted to know what they were eating, how we knew their names, and who had picked the scripture that was inside. Their excitement was too much. I had packed a million sack lunches for my kids, all with their names on them, and I had never seen this kind of energy over it. Jody and I asked if we could pray with the kiddos before they ate, and I could barely get through the prayers without big tears. When it was time to deliver the last class's lunches, we witnessed the same response from the students and asked if we could pray with them before they ate. We prayed. I choked back tears. And then a young boy asked if he could pray for us. Oh my word. He put his precious hands on us and prayed for our families. He prayed for us to be blessed. He thanked the Lord for the food we had provided. And tears mixed with snot rolled down my face. I would never be the same.

Jesus provided the amazing army of women to take lunches the rest of that fall. I was always floored by His provision. I was always shocked by how He could make things happen. And then I was always embarrassed by my lack of faith. Here was this Jesus who had walked me out of the woods and was so good—didn't I believe yet that He could do anything? He used those lunches again and again to show me His power. He could do so much with one little yes. He could move mountains if we just say yes. And here I was in awe of the fact that what

His word said was actually true, and this mustard seed of faith I possessed was worth so much more than just talking about doing good things on occasion for Jesus. This was the abundant life. This was the real path, and with this baby in my belly, who had turned my world upside down enough for me to ask Jesus what my life looked like through HIS eyes, I kept asking Him what He wanted from my life. And He just kept answering.

One afternoon, on a drive back from Generation One, I felt brave enough to tell Jody what I felt Jesus was asking me to do. I had begun that summer before organizing a once a month gathering of women where one woman would share her Jesus Story. We had done this a few times. I had wanted to do it just for the summer because now I was organizing this lunch army, and I was only getting more pregnant, but Jesus wouldn't let it go. Years before, even before I had taught in the Colt Academy, God had me look up my name, "Hooks," in the Bible. This took me to Micah 4:3 which speaks about the end of time when nations will come before God, lay down their weapons, and God will turn the weapons into plowshares and pruning hooks. The words "pruning hooks" struck me then. It struck me that God would take weapons and turn them into useful tools. And I would wonder for the next several years what Jesus had in store for those words in my life as I lay down weapon after weapon and all my anger, and He turned all of my life into a useful tool for Him.

So, that day in the car I told Jody possibly one of the longest stories and that finally I felt like I knew what pruning hooks was for. I felt the nights where women gathered together to hear one girl's Jesus Story, and the lunch teams that kept growing were part of this same place in my heart. I believed Jesus wanted me to start a ministry, Pruning Hooks, where everyday ordinary women could serve Jesus allowing their everyday ordinary lives to become extraordinary. I believed many women didn't know where to serve or didn't believe they had anything to offer, and God was asking me to give women opportunities to serve Him. I believed it would be more than just lunches someday. And I believed that the Jesus Stories of ordinary women would allow other women to see that Jesus is writing a story in all of our lives, no matter how ordinary we all felt. And I waited for Jody to tell me I was crazy. Instead, she told me that she thought it was so needed, and she thought women would be so thankful to finally have a place to serve Jesus and see Him work. Pruning Hooks Ministry began in the front seat of a minivan with a conversation between two Jesus-crazy women who were living on faith just enough to have a conversation that just might require another mustard seed.

Pruning Hooks started with a boatload of prayer, and some women. My crazy friends, Amber, Amy and Jody, prayed and listened and read the Bible. We were moved by songs. We were moved by church. We were moved by what Jesus was up to in the life of ordinary women, and Jesus was definitely doing extraordinary things. We began to make plans to deliver breakfast to the school starting in 2013. We began to make plans for groups of godly men to serve hot breakfast to Generation One Academy every Friday morning. We began to make plans to work with teen moms at a local high school. We began to make plans for a prom dress drive for teens with a chronic illness. We sold necklaces to raise money for orphans each month. We listened intently for opportunities all around us and were beyond excited whenever those opportunities led us to more chances to be the hands and feet of Jesus. We continued with Pruning Hooks nights the last Thursday of every month and watched women be moved by the stories of faith from a regular girl. Those nights were filled with the Holy Spirit reminding each of us we were not alone. And I began to anticipate with joy the birth of my fourth child, Joshua Clay Hooks. I had plans down to the minute of how I would manage everything with ease. I had a plan to please Him. And once again I took up my power point presentation prayer and began to show Jesus just how I thought this running a ministry and having my fourth baby should all work. And once again, Jesus reminded me that I was not listening; but I kept right on talking at Him, down to the last minute.

Joshua Clay Hooks was born a month early, on January 11, 2013. I went in for a routine appointment with my doctor and, due to his heart rate being abnormally high, was sent to the hospital instead. I was a mess. God had required me to abandon all my plans over and over and over again the past year, and now here I was abandoning more plans and being forced to trust in Him. I knew He was good. I knew He loved me. I knew He was working out every moment for good. But I was being forced to add to my list of facts showing how good and loving and faithful Jesus was, and I was tired. We were supposed to have the first group of guys cook hot breakfast on January 11, and I would not be there.

I was having to trust God for every painstaking plan we had made. I was about to meet my baby, Joshua, and I was scared to death. I was scared with him being a month early. I was scared with having to adjust to life with a baby again. I was scared to miss sleep. I was just scared. I was told we would most likely do an emergency c-section and was given the night to try to induce labor and monitor Joshua's heart rate. As I sat in the hospital room with my Bible, my cell phone filled with text messages, and my precious husband painting my toenails, I knew God had this. I knew He was right there in that room with all of us—me and Corey and Joshua. I knew His plan was bigger and better than mine ever could be, and throughout the night I witnessed the power of prayer.

My doctor slept in the hospital because she was so certain she would have to perform an emergency C-section. Joshua's heart rate would accelerate unbelievably with every teeny tiny contraction. By 3:30 a.m., as I prayed and did deep knee bends (don't ask, it just felt better than laying down), his heart rate was normal. Joshua responded to each contraction like a champ, and the nurses said it was a miracle. When my doctor came in at 6:00 a.m. to let me know there would be no need for emergency surgery, she pulled up a chair and suggested we talk about the gospel until she had to see her next patient. And so Joshua's little life was ushered in with super duper prayer, the love of the gospel, and my mom making it just in the nick of time to see a fuzzy-headed little boy take his first breath just as she had for the other three grandkids.

Jesus answered so many prayers, big and small, on January 11, 2013. Corey and I learned an unforgettable lesson that morning: When God gives you a reward trust that it will be rewarding. The moment I saw my itty bitty Joshua, I knew that if I had a glimpse of this moment the night I found out I was pregnant, I would have sprinted to the end of that amazing marathon to get the best prize ever.

Joshua Clay melted off the last pieces of ice on my heart. Joshua made me ooshy gooshy and snuggly with a tiny little infant who could not lift his head. With Joshua, God took sleepless nights and filled them with laughter and loads of pictures of my baby. I was smitten. I could not get enough. I was finished talking at God, and I was sold on obedience. I was sold on the obedience that changes everything. My family was changed. Corey was changed. The three older kids were changed. We were a tighter unit as we all dug in together to take care of this baby. Weapons were crashing all over the floor and being turned into pruning hooks in our lives. By that summer Joshua had spent more time at Generation One or with teen moms than most kids from Katy, Texas, do when they are a few months old. It was crazy, and everywhere we went people loved the baby. He was easy. (We needed an easy baby.)

The gals who started Pruning Hooks with me helped pick up the pieces of the puzzle to make sure the hands and feet of Jesus could keep working. It was unreal to watch Him work out every detail still. It was unreal to watch my kids become part of the plan. It was unreal to watch Him tie up so many loose ends on a daily basis, and just when I thought my head would explode, there He would be with a text or a prayer or a phone call or just the right gal at just the right time looking to serve Jesus.

In the mix of a new baby and running a ministry and loads upon loads of laundry, God said to write another Bible study. This time it was called "Salty," because we were not called to be sugar. We were called to be salt and make others thirsty for Jesus. He wanted our lives to look different. He wanted us to show other people Him, and we couldn't do it just by being nice enough, because Jesus wasn't "nice enough" either. He was this awesome living water, but before people wanted a drink, they had to get thirsty. And man oh man, salt makes you thirsty. If we weren't causing the people around us to get thirsty for Jesus, then our lives just weren't salty enough. And my life had gotten saltier over the past year. As surprised as

I was that He was asking me to write another Bible Study, this time, I simply said yes and got on about His business.

And that is pretty much how it kept on going. Teach the Bible Study and I will give you the place, He said. And a friend's father, whom I had never met, let us use an upstairs of his office building free of charge to teach "Salty," sleeping baby in tow. Help whomever I place in your path, He said. And I watched as this army of women grew and loved on single moms with meals, clothes, and groceries. We loved on children who were in foster care. We loved on teen moms trying to make it through school, and we loved on cancer patients with fun-filled meals once a month. It was incredible to see what Jesus could do with anyone's YES. It was unbelievable to see what the Body of Christ looked like when we just put our weapons at His feet and let Him change them into useful tools. And serving Him was so much fun. This was the abundant life. This was grace-filled living. This was what happened when you knew God was good and loved you even in your worst circumstances. You could simply know what He said was true and trust that He was working it all out. If He put a needy family in your path, you simply said yes to help them and knew He would work out the details. We never knew how He would work things out, but we always knew why we said yes. And the why of our yes really was all that ever mattered. There was a Carpenter King at work all the time, and He wanted people to come to know He was good, and we (and I mean all of us) were so often the only way others would know He loved them and He was good and He was working it all out for them too.

Each time we served someone new, Jesus would whisper:

This is how much I loved you that day in the woods. I was sending people your way. I was putting the right teachers at the right time into your classroom. I was making sure you had Judah and Jamie so you knew you were not alone living a crazy life. I sent you a picture of the entire gospel on the cover of a Bible so you could know I was holding you. I gave you a sister to stand in the darkness with you, and a sister to believe in you. I gave you Nashville for peace in the midst of every storm. I gave you a step-father who would turn your life around and teach you how to laugh again, and a mom who would finally surrender to me and change everything. I gave you a dad who just loved you, from far away or up close, and saw you always through the eyes of a dad, as precious and special. And you may have only thought people were being kind to you, but I was writing a love letter to you all over each day. I was stretching out my arms to you every single morning and hoping you would let me hold you. And here we are at the beginning of a very long road...not the end...just the beginning...a really really good beginning where weapons become useful tools, and little girls lost in the woods come out to dance in the sun.

CHAPTER 7

Shalom Y'all

So, this is peace y'all. This is the life I would never have imagined for myself. Really full. Really filled with kiddos and a husband and me, and we are so far from perfect. I often tell people, if you want to feel good about yourself then come to my house at 5 p.m. any day of the week and witness a woman at her wits end wrestling through homework and diapers and dinner and five million questions. It is not pretty, but man, it is good. This is the peace that I never knew was possible. Sitting down to dinner each night with my husband and four kids; starting the dinner prayer about twenty-eight times before everyone bows their heads; taking turns picking up the baby's cup off the floor; listening to different jokes of varying degrees of funny throughout the meal; hearing about a day at school; and talking about things that don't really matter—this is my dinner each night. It sometimes gets louder. Sometimes people are asked to leave the table because they are arguing with siblings or refusing to eat vegetables. We are a really typical crew; but we are filled with this crazy peace at the end of the day. At the end of the day when I crawl into bed with Corey and the whole house is quietish and we stare at a TV screen and watch something that has almost no redeeming qualities, I reach over, across the sleeping baby who has taken over eighty-eight percent of a king-size bed, and I grab Corey's hand. It's in that moment, I know that God is so big and so good and wants our lives to be filled to the very top with Him so much that it spills over onto everyone else.

It is in those semi-peaceful moments at the end of the day, when all the laundry that is going to get folded has been folded, and the dishwasher is humming away with a stack of dishes still in the sink—when the house is lit by a lamp or two and Corey is either yelling at the Rangers on TV or asleep with glasses still on his face...that is when I have feel absolute joy. This was the plan. It took me a long time to get to the plan, but this was the plan all along. This plan where I feel loved and cherished and give love and hugs generously. This plan where I am for real. This plan where my laughter and my jokes are not just a front, but a window into the joy of knowing Jesus Christ is good and He loves me. This is the joy of knowing there was a plan all along, and although I went in a million different horrible directions, the plan God had for my life was here waiting for me all along. This plan was for no one else. This plan was just for me.

And all four kiddos were part of this plan. And this crazy husband of mine was part of this plan too. And the people we have walked shoulder to shoulder with along this road, they were part of this plan. I can look back on my life from right here in a Starbucks and see how often Jesus tried desperately to put my feet upon His path. I can look back and see how many times I was so close to my Savior and just turned and walked another way. And to be honest, much of my childhood was stolen from me. To be honest, the majority of my youngest years were destroyed by people who were desperately trying to stay on their own path and keep far away from the path God had actually paved for them. It took years, and lots of prayer, and then some more prayer, but I have come to this place of forgiveness. Real forgiveness. I look at these people through the eyes of Jesus, and I see how heartbroken He is for them. I see how He wants so desperately to see them on the path He created for them since the beginning of time, and His heart for them softens my heart too, and I have been able to forgive and move on and move over and step on down this road without crazy amounts of anger tripping me up all the time.

And I would be lying to you if I didn't tell you that sometimes I try to walk backward on this road. I would be lying to you if I didn't tell you that there are still times I feel inexplicably terrified. The terror comes out of nowhere, and I feel the need to build an army bunker and throw my kids in there with some bottled water and canned goods to keep us all away from this fear that someone is going to steal them. I have to stop. I have to pray. I have to text Amy McGown for wisdom. I may have these moments for the rest of my life. But I am not building a bunker. I haven't locked my kids away. I am standing with Jesus way out in the light knowing He has a plan, and the plan doesn't include an underground hideaway because a sick man decided to steal my innocence over thirty years ago. That plan would never allow for me to see Jesus at work. I might be safe, but I would be without the knowledge of the miraculous goodness of my Jesus.

So, this is peace y'all. I get to live out the love of my Savior for other people in pain. I get to be part of His plan for His children that are hurting today and tomorrow too. I get to be part of His revelation to them that He sees them and knows them and is writing a love letter to them too. I get to be part of the reminder that God is good, and He loves them very much. As I deliver food, or prom dresses, or dinner or groceries or toiletries or gift cards with this random, rag tag army of women I get to see other people realize they are not alone. This is not a road about me anymore. This is a road about leading other people to the goodness of God. And He is so good y'all. And He is wanting other people to know, and He is stirring our hearts and shouting into to our lives, go and do and be my hands and feet to everyone you see. He is asking us to know the people we come in contact with daily, and do something, anything for the broken people all around us. Some days all you may have is a smile and a compliment, but it may be just the words that allowed one person to know that they are still important and loved and there is a path being paved for them too. This life, this crazy life He has offered me, reminds me that He sees me too. Only Jesus can take all your pain and use it to give others hope. Only Jesus can take the wrecked life of an ordinary girl and turn it into something extraordinary.

And can I tell you this? He wants to do the same for you too? Can I tell you He is waiting for your heart to collide with His plan for you, and you will never be the same? Can I tell you when He sees you He smiles? Can I tell you He thinks you are beautiful? Can I tell you the day you were created He couldn't wait to get you to the perfect plan He had created just for you? And you may have wandered. And you may have run the other direction. And you may have a million pounds of regret. And you may not know where to begin. But He is so ready to show you how He has been there all along. He is so ready to see your eyes open wide with the understanding that He has been with you every moment, and is fighting a mighty battle for you...just for you...because He loves you with all of His heart. He always has. He always will.

One day, this past school year, I was walking my kids to school. I had parked at my friend's house and we were walking all of our kiddos together to the crosswalk where they would, in turn, walk with the crossing guard across two streets and be on school grounds. (It's a little bit of freedom for the kids.) We do it every day. We stand their watching them, and the crossing guard walks with them the rest of the way, and they feel a little more independent. Most days this takes place without much pause. Occasionally, my kids are continuing an argument from the car, and we have the humiliating experience of working out our issues on the sidewalk. Occasionally, there are untied shoes, or running races, or pressing the walk button ninety-eight times, which will get them yelled at by the crossing guard. But most days are just days, and there is nothing special about this walk to school other than my conversation with my walking buddies. So, it caught me off guard this one particular day. Grace had been walking way slower than her two brothers. I must have said too many times to count for her to hurry up. She was actually stopping and picking flowers. When she finally caught up to us at the crosswalk, she informed me she had picked a handful of wild flowers for her teacher. I let her know that was wonderful. The light changed, I kissed her head and as she started to walk across the crosswalk, the fear hit like an avalanche.

Maybe it was because my walking buddy was not with me that day. Maybe it was because Grace's brothers had gone on ahead, and she was walking alone. And as I stood frozen in fear, I could see nothing except a movie in my head of someone jumping out of their car and grabbing my little angel. I could see them stealing her away, and I would never be able to save her, and I would have been so close, but there would be nothing I could do because this would be the painful plan I was supposed to live through. As this scenario clicked through my mind at rapid speed, I reached for the light post because I was trying not to run after her. I was digging down deep and trying to be some kind of normal mom that didn't live out horror stories in her head at eight o'clock in the morning while watching her daughter walk to school.

At just that moment where Grace was supposed to plant her foot on the other sidewalk she stopped. And Grace came running all the way back to me. Just at that moment when I couldn't take one ounce more of my fear and my nightmare, Grace bounded all the way back for me. She shoved the bouquet of wildflowers in my hand, and said she wanted me to have them instead. And as the crossing guard yelled warnings of how dangerous Grace's choice to turn back had been, my Grace planted a big old kiss on my face and grabbed my hand. I walked with her the entire way to school that day. I walked choking back buckets of tears. I walked with Grace right up to the front door and heard all about a little girl's plans for her day filled with happiness and friends and a mommy who walked her to school.

Those moments for me were filled with my Jesus. He was in that run across a street from my little Grace. He was in the eyes of my 7-year-old girl as she bounded through a crosswalk all smiles. He sent her back to me. She was running back to me. She had no doubt she had made the right decision. She didn't care about the risk. She cared about the person on the other side of the road. She had no idea about the small nervous breakdown happening inside of me, but Jesus knew.

In that crosswalk instant, I am not alone. In that instant, I am seen. In that instant, I am worth it. In that instant, I am wanted. In that instant, I am the most prized possession. In that instant, I am His. And I have been having these instances with Jesus all of my life. All of my life.

And you have too. He has been crossing all sorts of roads to get to you too. Because He knows you are having your own personal breakdown on a sidewalk, and He wants you to get to the good part. He wants you to get to the part where you are walking with Him. He wants you to get to the part where no matter what load you are carrying, you are carrying as the totally loved prized possession of the most High King. And your path may have some huge bumps and maybe even mountains up ahead, but He is not leaving. He is walking with you until this road is over. And along the way, you are going to have the chance to be His hands and feet running back for all the other people standing frozen at crosswalks on an ordinary Tuesday. Because Jesus is big y'all.

So, this is peace y'all. This is the good life. It is not glamorous. It is not filled full of riches and pony rides and easy living. It is simply filled full of Jesus. It is filled full of all the blessings He can fit into a life, and my favorite ones share my last name or used to share my last name or are the type of friends that are so close people think we share the same last night. This is the peace that accompanies a long journey, and realizing you get to breathe here and there, but there is still more to go because Jesus is not through with you yet. This is the peace that comes when you pull into your driveway and almost cry every time because of all the people waiting inside, and it is good y'all. So, this is peace. And no, it is not always peaceful, but it is peace-filled. And in the midst of chaos and craziness, I walk with my Jesus who has walked with me since the day I was born.

Shalom Y'all.

Made in the USA
San Bernardino, CA
01 March 2020